2

Table of Contents

4

Chapter 1

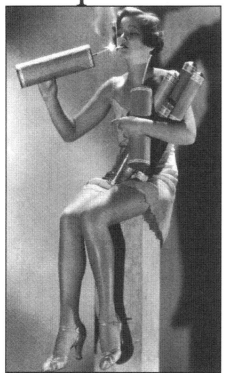

Defining Yourself and Setting Goals

6

Defining Yourself

In the end, who is responsible for your education? On the surface of it, this is a fairly simple question. But for many students, the people around them, including parents, siblings, instructors, employers and many others, have influenced their goals and either helped or hindered their progress towards those goals.

Your parents may have been supportive of the goals you have chosen or they may have been indifferent. They may have guided you in your goals and even directed you to choose a certain profession. Maybe your employer has been understanding of your goals and has supported your education. Or maybe your employer has asked you to work overtime when you have a difficult assignment or test the next day. Maybe you have had teachers and professors who have worked out well for you, but maybe you have had an instructor who was rude to you and would not listen to you. And maybe your little brother actually did eat your homework.

Many students in community colleges often find that they are doing something that the people around them do not understand or sympathize with. Students who come from high school often find that their friends have either moved on to universities or have entered the workforce. Students who return to college after several years of working or raising a family often feel alone or think they are the only ones coming back to school.

No matter what your situation, the one of the first things you need to do when you enter college is figure out why you are here. Some people know exactly why they are in college, what they want to accomplish and how they are going to get there. Most don't.

Taking an Active Role in Creating Yourself

Once you have decided to become a college student you have decided you want to accomplish something significant. You may have come to college with only a vague notion of what you want to achieve over the next few months and years, or you may have come to college with clear goals in mind and a set of firm expectations about what you expect to accomplish. Maybe you are somewhere in the middle of these two positions. No matter what you preparation level or your expectations you are making the decisions that affect who you become and the life you will one day look back upon with either regret or satisfaction.

You may have already heard that people with college degrees tend to have far better incomes over those people who do not hold college degrees. This is true. In fact, people with degrees tend to make about $10,000 to $20,000 more per year than people who do not hold them. People with college degrees also tend to spend far less of their life unemployed:

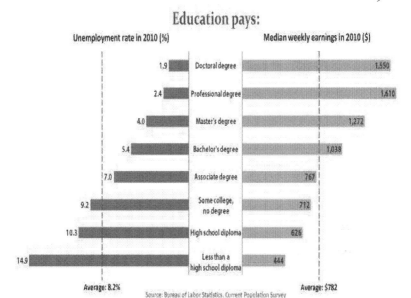

Education pays:

Unemployment rate in 2010 (%) — Median weekly earnings in 2010 ($)

Degree	Unemployment rate in 2010 (%)	Median weekly earnings in 2010 ($)
Doctoral degree	1.9	1,550
Professional degree	2.4	1,610
Master's degree	4.0	1,272
Bachelor's degree	5.4	1,038
Associate degree	7.0	767
Some college, no degree	9.2	712
High school diploma	10.3	626
Less than a high school diploma	14.9	444

Average: 8.2%   Average: $782

Source: Bureau of Labor Statistics, Current Population Survey

Source: http://www.bls.gov/emp/ep_chart_001.htm

But money alone is probably not a good reason to work so hard for a degree and give up so much along the way. You have probably heard that education is power, but it is not the kind of power that allows you to tell other people what to do. Instead being educated allows you to determine what you do with your life. Educated people decide what careers they go into and what they get to do with their lives. That kind of power over yourself is far more important that the ability to earn more money or tell other people what to do.

Taking the time to figure out what you want to do with the coming months and years and what you want to make of your life over the next few decades is essential to ensuring that you are the one who decides what becomes of your life.

10

There are plenty of people who would love to use your time and work to accomplish their goals. If you do not make these decisions about your future yourself, others will make them for you and they will have their interests, not yours, at heart.

Reflection 1-1

1. Do you have a good idea of what you want to accomplish in college? If not, do you have interests that you are considering?

_____

_____

_____

_____

_____

2. Who sets your agenda each day? Look over the tasks and duties you take care of each day and consider whose needs you are focusing on.

_____

_____

_____

_____

_____

3. How did you become interested in the goal you have set for yourself? Was there a person who influenced you or an experience?

_____

_____

_____

_____

_____

12

Staying Motivated

Being successful in college means being motivated throughout your studies. That seems simple enough, but keeping focused for the years it takes to finish your goals is not that easy. In the coming years, you are likely to encounter several obstacles as you work towards your goals. When someone or something interferes with you and your goals, it becomes more important than ever to stay focused on working towards the goals you have established for yourself. So many students find that the strain for balancing the demands of colleges studies with the demands of family, friends and work to be too much for them and they soon lose touch with the goals they set for themselves.

It is easy enough to understand that motivation is important, but many students find it difficult to stay motivated under the numerous pressures that are a part of completing college. Being motivated is not difficult when things are going well, but being a college student often means overcoming difficulties many others to not understand or help with. Many students run into difficulties with money, with their families or personal relationships and with their jobs. When these pressures mount up, staying focused on the work it takes to stay in college can seem impossible.

There may be classes you must take for your degree that just do not appeal to you, such as an economics or English course. There may be a personal tragedy in your life, such as an illness or a death of a family member that makes your college work seem far less meaningful. Motivation can fail even the most devoted students at times, but the difficulties you run into while working towards your degree should not keep you from completing the goals you have for your life. Being stubbornly attached to your goals becomes important at these times.

We tend to work hardest to protect and preserve those things that are truly ours. The goals you bring with you to college need to be truly yours, and when they are, you are far more likely to accomplish them.

It is not always possible to keep the troubles of the outside world out of your academic life, but if you have worked out your goals carefully and are truly dedicated to them, you are far more likely to get over the barriers fate and other people place in your way. Nearly all people who have been successful can tell of the careful plans they made and the difficulties they encountered along the way. Being studious and hardworking absolutely essential to becoming a good student, but being stubborn can carry you through times when life interrupts your plans.

Reflection 1-2

Directions: Take a moment right now and reflect on how your goals make you different from those around you, including your friends, family and co-workers. Consider whether these people understand your goals and whether they are helping you or distracting you.

_____

_____

_____

_____

_____

_____

_____

_____

_____

_____

_____

_____

_____

_____

_____

_____

_____

16

Planning Your Goals

Figuring out your academic and career goals is essential to being successful in college. Coming to college with the idea of taking a few classes to keep your parents happy is one of the most common strategies for failing out of college. Students come to college all the time with vague notions of what they want to do with their lives, and that's perfectly fine. You do not need to have goals set in stone right from the start, but you do need to start mapping out a strategy for the newt few years and base that plan on what you really want to accomplish in college and in your life.

You may have definite goals in mind with a clear academic and career path in mind. If you already know what your career goals are, making sure your academic path leads to these goals is usually not too difficult but it does take some time. You may be telling yourself that you have no idea about what you want to do in college. If you need to work out your primary goals for college and for your career, now is the time to begin thinking through the possibilities and challenges ahead.

Short-Term Goals

Completing your short-term goals involves managing the assignments and responsibilities you need to take care of over the next three months to one year. Doing this effectively involves setting priorities and managing the demands upon your time. Setting up your class schedule and completing the courses are the primary tasks for accomplishing your academic goals, but the demands of these classes need to be balanced with the demands your family and job place on our time.

The Need for Balance

Being a student in college today usually means balancing the different demands on your time and work in such a way that you can still move forward on your academic goals without losing touch with the other requirements you have to fulfill. But being a student often means taking a serious look at the demands other people are placing on your time and informing people that you can no longer meet their needs.

In many ways, being a student means being selfish. You have to place yourself and your own needs before the needs of others, often including employers and family members. In most cases, the conflicts between your needs to complete your college work and the needs of other can be managed. Informing your manager that you are working towards a degree and need to cut back on some of your workload or need to make changes to your work schedule is often effective. If an employer is not willing to accommodate your academic priorities, you might consider looking for a new position.

Accomplishing your goals in the coming years requires that you focus on your goals in the coming days, weeks and months. If you do not use your time to work towards your own goals, other people are ready and willing to take advantage of your time and work to accomplish their goals. The ability to tell people "no" is one of the most common characteristics of successful people because they are able to ensure that they can stay focused on their own goals rather than spending all their time responding to the demands of others.

Cutting back on time with friends and family is not always easy or possible, but managing your time with the people closest to you is often part of ensuring that things go more smoothly with them and with your studies. Cutting back on your time at work might also be necessary. You should consider how important your current job is to your intermediate goals when you are considering which one to sacrifice. Explain the importance of your studies and your goals to the people around you, and ask that they respect what you are undertaking. Family, friends and employers need to know what your goals are and need to understand the importance of your studies at this time in your life. Make it simple and clear that your time is currently quite limited.

Handling Distractions

The time and place you choose to study have a profound effect on how well you comprehend any reading materials. But finding a quiet place to study for the afternoon is not always possible for students with jobs and other responsibilities. And, oddly enough, it is not always the best way to study.

More important than peace and quiet is freedom from distractions. The most common distractions for college students are telephones, televisions and other people with requests and demands for your time. Getting time away from the distractions that take up so much of your day is essential to ensuring that your time is well spent when you are reading. Libraries are often excellent places to study, but they are not always the best choice for all students. The silence is often an inducement to take a nap rather than read a book or study a textbook chapter. For some people, the library can be an excellent location, but for others a coffeehouse or some place with bright lights and a little background noise might be better.

Many of the distractions we fact today are, ironically enough, made up of those inventions that are supposed to make our lives easier. Cell-phones and computers provide efficient and powerful tools for communicating with others and for completing work, but they often allow other people to interrupt our work or, even worse, allow us to distract ourselves from the assignments we need to complete. Keep these distractions under control by switching them off when you can or by putting some kind of barrier between you and the devices ability to distract you.

Reflection 1-3

Directions: Answer the following questions in detail.

1. Describe the time and place you are reading this book. Are you in between work and class or other responsibilities? Have there been any distractions?

_____

_____

_____

_____

2. Where do you usually study? Describe the time and place in detail.

_____

_____

_____

_____

3. What are your biggest distractions while studying? (Friends, phone, iPod?).

_____

_____

_____

4. What can you do to limit the effects of these distractions?

_____

_____

_____

_____

22

Scheduling for Success

During the first semester many students experience a bit of a culture shock. In high school, much of your day is already organized for you. You have a schedule that has been set for you from the morning and into the afternoon and takes up some 30 or so hours per week.

In college, you get to set your own schedule. You can be a full-time student but be in class fewer than 12 hours per week. That seems nice until you realize how much work has to be done outside of class. In most cases, you will need two hours outside of class for every hour you spend in class. In easy classes it might be less, but in more difficult classes it could be much more. So if you are in class for 12 hours per week, you need to set aside another 24 hours or so for study time. That 12-hour schedule becomes a 36-hour schedule once the study time is factored in.

Most students can handle a 36-hour schedule if it is set up for them, but when they have to set it up for themselves, it is often quite difficult, especially when there are other pressing responsibilities such as work and family. If you are working 30 to 40 hours per week on top of taking 12-units of class work, you have anywhere from 66 hours to 76 hours of responsibilities being placed on you outside of those you already have at home. Some people can handle such a schedule if they have supportive people around them and the resources they need, but most people cannot. They end up running into trouble at work, school and home when the competing responsibilities clash with each other.

24

   Working a full-time job, raising children and taking a full load of classes is
not likely to allow you to have much academic success. Many students have
thought they could accomplish it all, but have found studies in college or
relationships at home or work suffer. An overloaded schedule is most likely to
produce a good deal of stress and frustration and will ultimately lead to failure.

Exercise 1-1

Directions: Fill in the following chart with a realistic schedule of your weekly responsibilities. Put down your class times, study times, work times and any other responsibilities that you take care of each week:

	Sunday	Monday	Tuesday	Wednesday	Thursday	Friday	Saturday
6:00 AM							
7:00 AM							
8:00 AM							
9:00 AM							
10:00 AM							
11:00 AM							
12:00 PM							
1:00 PM							
2:00 PM							
3:00 PM							
4:00 PM							
5:00 PM							
6:00 PM							
7:00 PM							
8:00 PM							
9:00 PM							
10:00 PM							
11:00 PM							

Hours in class each week _____ Hours set aside for studying _____

Hours at work _____ Hours for other responsibilities _____

26

Intermediate Term Goals

Your intermediate term goals are those you plan to accomplish over the next one to four years. They are most closely tied to what you want to make of yourself professionally, but are usually built on what you need to do academically. For instance, if your career goal is to become a nurse, you need to plan the next two to four years on the course work you will need to accomplish.

With intermediate term goals, planning is the key. This means taking a good deal of time thinking through what you want to do with your life and how you can get there. The first step involves thinking seriously about what you want to be doing five to ten years from now. Take a good deal of time and consider which careers might interest you and keep you motivated. Some people might tell you what you should do, but in the end you really have to make your own decision since you are the one who will have to live with what you decide.

Much of the advice you have probably received has probably involved the practicality of your goals, and this is very important to consider, but if you have a goal in mind that others might consider unreasonable, you might not give up on it just yet. Some careers are very difficult to break into. Becoming a professional athlete or actor, for example, is not something many people accomplish. The number of people who never accomplish such goals is many times longer than the list of people who have ever made it to the big leagues or to Hollywood, but many people who pursue such goals often end up in related careers, such as coaching, teaching or managing others in the same field. A dedicated athlete can often become a coach, physical therapist or manager in the very same sport and enjoy that career as much if not more than they imagined.

If you are not sure of what you want to accomplish in the years to come, take the time to determine the characteristics of the type of position you would like and then try to figure out different possible academic and careers paths.

Types of Degrees

There are a number of degrees you can earn from a college or university. In most cases, you do not have to decide which level you want to work towards right away, but understanding the levels might help you plan out your academic and career goals in more detail.

Certificates

Certificates are not degrees but certifications from the state that you have satisfied a set of requirements for proficiency within a certain field and are now ready to work in a specific profession. There are usually few or no general education requirements for certificates, which means that courses in English, math or other fields are rarely required. Certificates are, instead, focused on preparing students for a profession, such as a firefighter, beautician, mechanic or nursing assistant, where college-level writing and mathematical skills are not always necessary.

The benefits of working towards a certificate are that you can complete the required courses more rapidly than the required courses for most degrees, and the certificate usually prepares you to enter a career soon after you have completed it.

Many fields require a certificate for entry-level positions, but advancement to management positions is often dependent upon achieving a higher level of education. To become a firefighter, for example, you must complete a set number of courses on safety and procedures directly related to the position, but to become a captain or chief, you need to have a college degree.

Associate of Arts/Associate of Science

The Associate of Arts (A.A.) and the Associate of Science (A.S.) degrees are the first level degrees you can earn at a community college. Earning one indicates that you have taken a required number of courses in a wide variety of fields such as English, math, sociology, history and the sciences, while you have also completed a number of courses towards your major.

The benefits of an A.A. or an A.S. degrees are that it does not take very long to earn, usually two to four years, but it ensures that you have a broad understanding of different areas of learning and also have specific skills related to your career choice. The idea behind the A.A. and A.S. degrees is that students learn about their choice of major but also have a well-rounded education that would allow them to analyze situations more effectively and communicate more clearly than someone without the advanced course work. Employers know that applicants with an A.A. or A.S. degree tend to have stronger reading, writing and mathematical skills than other applicants without such degrees.

The only difference between the A.A. degree and the A.S. is where the major fits into the colleges programs of study. Certain majors, such as English, theater and music, are awarded A.A. degrees, while other majors, such as biology, accounting and mathematics are awarded A.S. degrees.

Bachelor of Arts/Bachelor of Science

The Bachelor of Arts (B.A.) And the Bachelor of Science (B.S.) degrees are usually considered to be four-year degrees. These degrees are based on the general education requirements that are also covered in the A.A. and A.S. degrees, but they involve many more courses dedicated to your major.

The B.A. or B.S. degree usually require at least four years of study to complete, but many students take five or six years and sometimes even longer to complete their degrees. The students who take longer are often balancing demands at their jobs or with their family while pursuing their studies. The B.A. or B.S. degree opens professional opportunities often not available to those with certificates or associates degrees. Entry and advancement in many careers and management positions is often dependent upon the completion of a bachelor's degree.

The same basic distinction between the A.A. and the A.S. applies to the B.A. and B.S. degrees. If someone else tells you that one degree is better than the other, he or she is mistaken.

Teaching Credential

The teaching credential is required of most kindergarten through high school teachers and usually takes a year to complete. It is undertaken after the bachelor's degree is completed. Students receive intensive training in teaching methods and usually are given the opportunity to work with an experienced teacher.

Advanced Master and Doctorate Degrees

At this point in your studies, it is best to focus on earning a certificate, associate's or bachelor's degree before considering any more advanced studies. Master's degrees and doctorate degrees come after the bachelor's degree, but beginning these degrees is probably more than four years off, which places them beyond the range of setting intermediate goals. It is also important to have a few years of experience at the college or university level before setting your sights on these more advanced degrees.

Researching Your Degree Plans

Take the time to research what it takes to gain entry into a career and discuss what people in the career feel is necessary to be successful. In many fields, an entry-level degree, such as a certificate, an A.A. or an A.S., is all that is required. In many other areas, a higher degree is necessary to gain entry or to advance to a more advanced position.

If you are not sure of your academic and professional goals, you should not consider yourself lost, but you should apply yourself to moving in a certain direction. A good place to start is a counseling office on your campus. Taking the time to discuss your interests with a counselor can be quite helpful. Taking the time to flip through the numerous college and university catalogs can also give you a good idea of what majors and careers are available.

32

Exercise 1-2A

(For Certificate, A.A. or A.S. Students)

Directions: Answer the following questions using the college's catalogue.

    1.   Which major and degree do you plan on pursuing?

              _____

    2.   Does the college offer your major? Are there other degrees in

              your major? (For example, there might be three different nursing

              degrees offered.)

              _____

              _____

              _____

    3.   Which courses are required by the colleges for all A.A. or A.S.

              students? (These are usually general education requirements.)

              _____

              _____

              _____

              _____

              _____

34

4. Which courses are required for your major by the college?

   (These are usually courses that are specific to the major.)

   _____

   _____

   _____

   _____

   _____

5. Which courses have prerequisites?

   (Be sure to check *all* courses, not just English and math courses.)

   _____

   _____

   _____

   _____

   _____

Exercise 1-2B

(For transfer students)

Directions: Answer the following questions using a college's or university's catalogue.

1. Which major and degree do you plan on earning?

   _____

2. Which colleges or universities offer your major?

   (Try to find three or more.)

   _____

   _____

   _____

3. Which courses are required by one of the colleges or universities for all

   B.A. or B.S. students? (These are usually general education

   requirements.)

   _____

   _____

   _____

   _____

   _____

4. Which courses are required for your major by the college or university? (These are usually courses that are specific to the major.)

_____

_____

_____

_____

_____

5. Do you need to complete your A.A. or A.S. degree before transferring?

_____

6. Which courses do you need to complete before transferring? (These usually include general education, pre-requisites and lower division courses.)

_____

_____

_____

_____

_____

Exercise 1-3

(For all students)

Directions: Use a college catalogue and the previous exercise to fill in the education plan for the next two to four years.

Education Plan

First Year

First Semester   Second Semester

_____   _____

_____   _____

_____   _____

_____   _____

_____   _____

Second Year

First Semester   Second Semester

_____   _____

_____   _____

_____   _____

_____   _____

_____   _____

Third Year

First Semester   Second Semester

_____   _____

_____   _____

_____   _____

_____   _____

_____   _____

Fourth Year

First Semester   Second Semester

_____   _____

_____   _____

_____   _____

_____   _____

_____   _____

_____   _____

Talking to Those Who Know

No matter what career you have in mind, it is a good idea to discuss your plans with people who have already followed these paths. Most people are flattered to have someone discuss their careers with them, but do not be surprised if some are not so willing to speak with you. Find someone else.

Make sure you discuss both positive and negative aspects of the career. No career is enjoyable and rewarding all of the time. Teachers, for example, often find it quite rewarding to work with students and to see them grow intellectually over time, but many teachers find dealing with discipline issues, demanding parents and paperwork to be overwhelming at times. Many mechanics enjoy working with their hands and hearing an engine run just right, but dealing with customers and state regulations can take away much of the satisfaction of the career.

You should be careful to ask about the different areas of expertise that exist within the same career field. In many fields, there are different positions that have very different characteristics. Some areas of nursing take about three years of trying and do not require a bachelor's degree, while other areas require a master's degree or more. Nurses can work in such varied settings as emergency rooms, neonatal wards or even patients' homes.

Come up with a series of questions that allow you to get a better idea of what is involved in working in this area. Try to ask about the responsibilities, workloads, rewards and drawbacks. Make sure you understand how much education and experience are needed. Also see if there are related fields that might suit you, your temperament and your objectives best.

If you know someone in the field you are interested in, then your job is fairly simple. Contact them and discuss your questions with him or her. If you do not know someone already, take some time to find out who might be a good person to talk to. Instructors can often be good people to talk to, and they often know whom else you might contact. Avoid being either shy or overly aggressive. Be polite and persistent. Most professionals enjoy talking about what they do, but some might be less receptive or even rude to your request for their time. Do not be discouraged. If one person does not cooperate, another person will.

Exercise 1-4

Directions: Prepare for the interview by answering the following questions and writing up questions you feel are important.

1. Who is the person you are going to interview? What is their position or occupation?

   _____

2. What are five questions you would like to ask?

   1._____

   _____

   2._____

   _____

   3._____

   _____

   4._____

   _____

   5._____

   _____

(Be careful with taking notes during the interview. You might want to treat this as a discussion rather than a formal interview. The questions you initially ask could bring up other interesting issues you might want to ask about. Being either too formal or too casual would be a mistake in most cases. You might consider this a professional discussion. Be polite, be respectful, and, of course, be on time.)

42

Reflection 1-4

Directions: Write up a summary of what you have learned from the interview and how you plan to use what you have learned.

_____

_____

_____

_____

_____

_____

_____

_____

_____

_____

_____

_____

_____

_____

_____

_____

_____

Long Term Goals

Long term goals are those goals you have set for five to 20 years from now. These goals are distant enough to allow you to hope for a better situation than you are currently living in, but they tend to be so distant that they often seem more like vague wishes dependent more upon luck or fate than upon your own diligence and planning.

The difficulty with setting such goals is that they are contingent upon your reaching your intermediate term goals. You also need to keep your life from taking any unanticipated turns in direction. That is not easy to do. Most people encounter major changes in their living situation at one point or another over the decades. Moving, getting married, and having children are just a few of the events that can change your long-term plans. Other events, such as a divorce or a death of someone close to you can make accomplishing your long-term goals difficult.

In many instances, it is impossible to prevent these changes in the direction of your life from occurring, but if you have planned your intermediate goals carefully and have managed your short-term goals well, the changes that you experience over the long term are not likely to ruin the goals you have established for yourself but are more likely to require that you make adjustments to your goals. The important thing is to have well-thought out plans in place and to be following through on them daily, monthly and yearly. If you have your plans in place, the changes you encounter will be more manageable.

44

Reflection 1-5

Speak with someone who is over 40 years old about how they got to where they are

today. Did they know their life was going to take the direction it took? How well

were things planned in his or her life and how well did they accomplish their

goals? How much did good or bad luck affect the course of his or her life?

_____

_____

_____

_____

_____

_____

_____

_____

_____

_____

_____

_____

_____

_____

_____

_____

_____

46

Working on Your Goals

Working on the details of your academic plans starts with finding out what courses you need to take to complete your goals. Having some idea of what you need to complete or listening to what a friend may have done is a good way to waste your time on courses you do not need and to end up never finishing your goals for college.

Once you have some idea of what career you would like to go into and have some idea of how much education is required for the field or position, you need to make a detailed plan of how you are going to get through the required courses for your college degree or degrees.

If you plan on transferring to a four-year college or university, the first place to start is a catalogue from a college or university you are interested in attending. A good way to start working on your college plans is to read your college's catalogue and determine which courses you are going to need to complete your education. If you plan to transfer, find a catalogue of at least one of the colleges you might attend and determine what is needed to enroll in the college and complete your degree. You need to go through two different areas of the catalogue when you are planning to transfer.

1. First figure out the basic requirements for admission to the college or university. There should be a section that discussed the basic admission requirements for all students. Issues such as core math and English courses and GPA are usually covered in this area.

48

2. Then figure out the specific requirements for admission to your major. In most cases, the requirements for a specific major are slightly different than those for the college or university. An engineering major, for example, going to a university would probably need to take additional math classes beyond the basic requirements for the college or university before transferring, while the English major might need to take additional literature or composition courses before transferring to the same university. In most cases, four-year colleges and universities do not require that you complete your A. A. or A.S. before transferring. Knowing this could allow you to work on only what is needed for the B.A. or B.S. degrees.

3. Finally, figure out the graduation requirements for your major. This means finding out exactly which courses are needed to complete your degree. You do not want any surprises when you start working on your degree, especially because misunderstandings are quite common and can set back your goals significantly. You might also be able to streamline your time in college by taking required courses at the community college where they tend to be far less expensive.

If you plan on earning your certificate or degree at the community college, take the time to look through the two different areas of the catalogue.

1. First figure out what the graduation requirements are for the college. There are usually general education requirements for all students at the college. Even accounting majors, for example, need to complete a basic psychology course and usually more than one English composition course. If you are completing a certificate program, you probably do not need to worry too much about the college's requirements for graduation.

2. Then figure out which courses are required for your major or your certificate. Make sure you know exactly which courses are required and what the prerequisites might be. Many English and math courses, for example, have placement exam requirements o previous course work as prerequisites. And courses outside of English and math often have English and math courses as prerequisites. History courses, for example, often require students to finish certain English courses before allowing students to taking the courses, while physics courses often require students to finish certain math courses prior to taking the courses. You do not what to find these things out when it is too late.

If you have not seen a counselor at the college already, make an appointment to do so now. Right now. But do not put off your planning until you see the counselor. If you have already done a good deal of work on your goals and understand many of the issues and requirements before you see the counselor, your meeting should go far better. You will be able to ask better questions and the counselor will be able to provide more detailed and useful advice for you.

Exercise 1-5

Directions: Evaluate the problems or threats to your goals and consider how you will respond to these challenges.

I. Short-term goals:

A. What are the potential threats to your goals for the next three months? (Consider scheduling issues and the demands placed on your time.)

_____

_____

_____

_____

_____

B. What are the potential threats to your goals for the next year? (Consider the potential for changes in your work and family arrangements. What should be happening and what will you do if things do not go according to the original plan.)

_____

_____

_____

_____

_____

_____

II. Intermediate Term Goals

A. In two years. What should you have accomplished in college after two years? Cover the goals you have for your home and work. Consider changes that should be taking place.

_____

_____

_____

_____

_____

_____

_____

B. Two years. What are the biggest threats to your plans for the next two years? What can you do to eliminate, minimize or adapt to these threats?

_____

_____

_____

_____

_____

_____

_____

C. Three to four years. Where do you want to be in three to four years?

What are the other possible scenarios that may develop in this time?

_____

_____

_____

_____

_____

_____

_____

_____

54

Vocabulary Development

Part of developing your vocabulary involves learning the essential parts of many of words. Most of the vocabulary you learn at the college level comes from word parts that originated in Greek or Latin. Once you learn the lists of word parts, you will find that you can figure out many more words.

Learning the lists of word structure parts cannot be done by reading over the page once or twice. This would be an easy way to forget the definitions within a day or two. Instead, they should be written down on flash cards and memorized. The prefix or root should be written on one side and the definition and an example should be written on the back.

Here is an example of the front and back of one card:

Eu

Good, well.

Eugenics, eulogy, euphemism

Each chapter includes a word structure list. Place these word structure parts on cards as you work your way through the book and keep the cards for review.

Word Structure List 1

Exercise 1: Turn the following Greek and Latin word parts into flash cards. Put the word structure part on one side and the definition with an example on the back.

1. a, an–not, without. Examples: anemia, anonymous.

2. ab–away, away from   Examples: abnormal, absent.

3. bel/bell–war Examples: rebel, belligerent, antebellum

4. bi–two. Examples: bilateral, bicycle.

5. bio–life. Examples: biology, biography.

6. cap/cip/cept–to take, to get   Examples: capture, anticipate, precept.

7. chron–time. Examples: chronograph, chronicle.

8. circum–around. Examples: circumference, circumnavigate.

9. cand–to burn Examples: candle, incandescent, candor.

10. cap/capit/cipit–head Examples: capital, captain, precipitate.

11. dict–speak. Examples: dictator, dictation.

12. dog/dox–opinion Examples: orthodox, paradox, dogmatic.

13. don/dot/dow–to give   Examples: donate, donor, endow.

14. fid–faith, trust Examples: confide, different, affidavit.

15. fin–end Examples: final, confine, define.

16. mort–death. Examples: mortgage, mortician.

17. multi–many. Examples: multiply, multinational.

18. neo–new. Examples: neoconservative, neonatal.

19. pan–across, all. Examples: pandemic, panacea.

20. path–feeling, pain. Examples: sympathy, pathology.

21. sen/sent–feel, think. Examples: sentimental, sentient. ,

22. sept–seven. Examples: Septuagint, September.

23. sex–six. Examples: sextet, sexpartite.

24. val–strong. Examples: valiant, value.

25. ver–true. Examples: verify, version.

58

Word Parts Exercise 1

Directions: Underline the Greek or Latin word part and give a definition of the Greek or Latin word part. Do not define the word.

1. _____ anemia   _____ finality
2. _____ bellicose   _____ multiples
3. _____ circumvent   _____ neonatal
4. _____ orthodoxy   _____ sensual
5. _____ fidelity   _____ capitulate
6. _____ verify   _____ sextet
7. _____ valor   _____ abhorrent
8. _____ endowment   _____ dictation
9. _____ September   _____ candle
10. _____ pathogen   _____ sentence

60

Chapter 2

The Reading and Learning Processes

62

Learning How to Learn

One surprise for many students when they start college is that the professors expect them to learn the material on their own. Much of what you are held responsible for learning is college is not covered in class. This means that you become the one who is responsible for teaching yourself most of the material you are required to learn in college. In a very real way, you need to split yourself into two different people: one who sets up lessons and learning environments and one who practices and rehearses the material. Knowing how to read the more difficult materials that you will encounter in college and knowing how your memory works are essential to understanding how to go about teaching yourself the difficult materials.

The Process of Problem Solving

Breaking problems down into manageable parts and solving them through a process are essential strategies for dealing with difficult tasks. The first stage requires that your break any assignment or problem down into its components. Try to identify tasks that can be completed in reasonable amounts of time at the start of the project. If you can plan out all the later stages of a project, do so. Knowing how much time and effort each stage is going to take makes the process easier to follow, but do now worry too much if the later stages are not clear from the beginning. The nature of the later stages of a longer project is often not clear until the earlier stages are well under way. As the later stages of a project becomes clear, take some time to plan them out and to manage your time appropriately.

Being able to plan out assignments and projects is one of the most important skills a student learns while in college. For many students, college is the first opportunity many students have to practice planning out their own schedules and own projects. Not knowing how to do this or failing to follow through on plans creates numerous difficulties for so many students and leads to frustration and frequently to failing classes and even dropping out of college.

If there is one characteristic marker of a successful student, it is the ability to make manageable plans while in college and to follow through on those plans in a methodical manner. Students who have financial burdens and other responsibilities that make being a dedicated student difficult often obtain better planning skills than those other students who do not have to confront these difficulties. Planning becomes a necessity if not a matter of survival.

The reasoning behind breaking assignments down into stages or steps is that the smaller divisions of a larger problem or project are easier to manage and more readily comprehensible. Nearly all difficult problems can be divided into segments. The overall problem or project might be daunting, but each segment can be worked out and resolved.

Purpose of Reading

Why do you read? Your answer to this question changes each time you read. When reading the directions on the back of a box of cold medicine, you probably read with an attention to detail to make sure you take the proper amount and at the proper intervals. When you are reading a magazine article in the dentist's office, you have a very different purpose in mind and may or may not be careful enough to read the entire article. Your appointment with the doctor or dentist probably takes precedent over the article.

When you are reading in college your purpose is different and your approach needs to be different each time you undertake a reading. The complexity and length of your readings in college are going to require that you develop a more sophisticated approach to the materials if you are going to be successful at learning the various subjects you are going to study.

College reading materials place a much greater demand upon your reading skills than the directions on the back of a cold medicine box or the articles in the magazines at your dentist's office. The assigned readings and textbook chapters you come across in college are more demanding than just about anything else you have read or will ever read. They often require that you focus your attention for a longer period of time and retain both the details and the main points with far greater accuracy than you are probably used to.

Learning the materials requires that your memory translate what you are reading on the page into a form that it can store and recall later. Your memory does not work like a computer, but it does require that you follow certain procedures if it is going to remember the more difficult material you are reading in college.

66

Reflection 2-1

1. What are your college reading assignments this week?

_____

_____

_____

_____

2. What are the purposes of each reading? Consider what you expect from the readings but also what the instructor wants you to learn from each one.

_____

_____

_____

_____

_____

3. How do you plan to ensure that you have learned the material in each reading assignment?

_____

_____

_____

_____

_____

_____

68

How Memory Works

Memory is at the heart of learning, and developing your memory is about knowing which learning strategy to use in which situation. Certain materials can be learned most effectively using certain strategies, while other materials can be learned most effectively using entirely different strategies. Learning the words for a vocabulary test, for example, is entirely different from preparing a difficult reading for an essay exam in history.

In some cases, the learning task is a matter of memorizing details, while in others the details are not as important as comprehending the complicated relationships that hold a number of events and ideas together. Then there are the formulas and other processes that require memorization and an ability to apply what you have memorized. Each situation requires a different approach and different strategies. Understanding how to learn and when to apply certain strategies makes your study time far more efficient and effective.

Reflection 2-2

1. Do you consider yourself to have a good memory? Are some things easier to remember than other things?

_____

_____

_____

_____

_____

2. When it is important to remember something, what do you currently do?

_____

_____

_____

_____

_____

3. Do you find it difficult to recall information during tests?

_____

_____

_____

_____

_____

72

The Mechanics of Memory

Psychologists have constructed models of how memory functions on a number of levels. These models really describe how the memory functions rather than how it is constructed physically within the brain. Your memory functions in an efficient manner and saves space by forgetting far more than it remembers. It also tries to structure information and strategies in such a way that make them easier to recall and apply to the world.

Memory is not a simple matter of storing what you see or read. There are certain procedures and methods that work better with different types of materials and information that need to be learned. You memory has a number of different levels that have to be considered when you are trying to learn new material.

Sensory Memory

At the first level is the sensory memory which deals with what is needed to sustain the senses and their communications with your mind. Whenever anything is perceived through the senses, part of your memory is used to hold the image, sound, smell or other sense in the mind for the briefest of moments.

When you are driving your car or taking a walking down a busy street, for example, you see and hear an enormous number of sensory inputs and these inputs are flashed into your memory for a very, very short time so that the other images and sounds can come into your attention. The trees and fire hydrants are easily forgotten soon after they are seen while you concentrate on the more important signs from cars and traffic signals.

To a degree you are in control of what your sensory memory focuses on, but often you are not. If you are crossing a street on foot, you can focus on the lights and watch for the sign to cross the street, but if a car's horn blows, you have no choice but to pay attention. Your attention is immediately drawn to the sound of the horn.

Keep in mind that the sensory information is translated into a form that can be registered temporarily in your memory. The things you see, the sounds you hear, and the odors you smell are usually not stored in your more permanent memory in a way that you can recall. Instead all this information is translated into neurological signals that your brain can understand for a matter of moments.

Nearly all of this information that you take in while driving to the college or crossing the street is forgotten. Much of the forgetting takes place at night when you are sleeping. Your brain cleans out much of the information it took in. And that is a good thing. You do not need to remember the color of a car you passed on the way to the college three weeks ago. Such information would simply clutter your memory and make it more difficult to recall and use the information and knowledge you need to function throughout each day.

Reflection 2-3

1. What did you have for breakfast this morning?

   _____

   _____

2. What did you have for breakfast yesterday?

   _____

   _____

3. What did you have for breakfast 10 days ago?

   _____

   _____

4. If you forgot what you had for breakfast yesterday or ten days ago, what do you think is happening to your memory over the course of 10 days? Why would you forget or be able to remember?

   _____

   _____

   _____

   _____

   _____

   _____

   _____

   _____

76

Working Memory

The next level of memory is referred to as working memory or short-term memory. You may have heard of short-term memory before, but were unclear about what it really is. Today psychologists often refer to short-term memory as working memory since there is far more to it than the brief duration it lasts when compared to long term memory. Working memory is where your mind holds onto certain information and ideas and works through any applications or problems it needs to solve.

To work through a math problem, for example, you needs to have the various numbers and symbols in your memory during the process and then you need to rework them according to the new and old principles of mathematics that are learning or have learned some time ago. Once you have completed the problem, these numbers and concepts begin their retreat from your working memory while you concentrate on the next problem. In the end, it is not the time span of working memory that is important but its ability to hold onto both information and concepts while working with them in a variety of ways.

The bad news is that you have a limited amount of working memory available, and its capacity is pretty much determined at birth. No matter how much you study and learn, you cannot increase the capacity of your working memory. Oddly enough students do not need an above average working memory capacity to be successful in college. The ability to manage how you use your working memory is far more important than the capacity of working memory to handle complicated tasks.

Managing working memory becomes important since only so much working memory space is available at any time. Most people cannot, for example, work on a difficult algebra or calculus problem while following an interesting movie on television. It takes too much working memory to think through the stages of the mathematical problem while following the plot and dialog of a movie that engrosses your attention. When you overload your working memory, it starts to bog down and function less effectively.

Reflection 2-4

1. When do you tend to be most focused? While driving in difficult conditions, while participating in an athletic event, while performing at church or any other occasion?

_____

_____

_____

_____

2. What kinds of distractions come up at these times, and how do you deal with them?

_____

_____

_____

_____

3. Do you ever get annoyed when someone breaks your concentration at an important moment? Why do you think this occurs?

_____

_____

_____

_____

_____

80

Long Term Memory

Long-term memory is much closer to what you probably already consider to be memory. Long-term memory involves the storage of memories of facts, images and impressions, but it is also where you store more complicated processes and procedures. The good news is that your long-term memory is basically limitless and it is also where most real learning takes root. Developing your long-term memory is what higher level learning is about, and making ideas and concepts stay is what the most effective study strategies do.

The difficult task is to figure out the most effective ways to have the information and concepts that are essential to your education take root in your memory. This does not happen naturally, especially if there are a number of distractions going on in your learning environment. Developing your memory is not easy and there are no "tricks" you can use to memorize large amounts of information or difficult theorems, but there are strategies that work far more effectively than others.

Memory development might seem like a complicated subject, but in the end there are three basic ways we remember things:

1. Patterns

2. Repetition

3. Unusual or emotional events

Anything lodged in your memory and readily retrievable has a recognized pattern, has been repeated a number of times or struck you as extraordinary or emotionally charged.

Your memory cannot possibly hold onto all the sensory information, conversations and ideas you come across in a single day, let along an entire semester. What the brain does to deal with the overload of information you come across in any day to forget nearly everything that strikes it as unimportant. This process of forgetting is done without any conscious effort on your part. In fact, trying to forget something usually does not work well.

Much of the cleaning of your memory slate is done at night when you are sleeping, and, unfortunately, much of what is swept away includes the materials you read in your textbooks and hear during lectures. The primary targets for removal are the information and ideas that have not been reinforced through repetition, that have no recognizable and memorable structure or that have nothing strikingly unusual or emotional about them.

The tie your professor might or not wear is something you would probably forget quite readily. Your professor probably does not wear the same tie every day, and most people do not consider ties to be something to get too emotional about. But what if he did wear the same tie for a week? Do you think you would be able to describe it the next week? What if he always a serious person and tended to wear drab colors, but then he showed up to class with a brightly colored suit and a tie with cartoon characters on it? The novelty of it would probably make the tie and even the suit more memorable, and you would probably be able to describe it a week or more after he wore it. And what if he wore a suit where the colors were contrasting but worked quite well together?

So what does this mean when you are preparing for a mid-term examination on Moby Dick or the Civil War? The type of task you have to complete should determine the strategy you use. When there are lists of items to be memorized and the list does not have a readily apparent structure, relying on repetition is usually the best method. Remembering definitions of many words, for example, can be done with flash cards that can be practiced repeatedly. Reading through the list of words once or twice does not reinforce the information well enough.

When working with longer readings, the goal is not accurate memorization but comprehension of the ideas and their relationship to each other. Reading the assignment repeatedly would not be practical in most cases and would not be effective. Instead, the goal should be to uncover and comprehend the structure of the material. Understanding how an essay or chapter in a textbook is structured and how the ideas relate to each other is far more effective and takes far less time than trying to read something more than once.

84

Reflection 2-5

1. Take a look over some of your academic demands on you this week, such as preparing for a vocabulary quiz in business or an in-class essay for history. Do they seem like tasks that need to be repeated or structured?

_____

_____

_____

_____

2. Did you ever need to memorize a poem or part for a play? Were you ever part of a team and needed to memorize a number of formations or strategies? How did you go about ensuring that you were ready when the time came to recall the material?

_____

_____

_____

_____

3. You probably have certain areas of expertise and certain areas where you need to develop expertise. Why do you think it is easier to learn about unfamiliar topics?

_____

_____

_____

_____

86

Reading Process

The reading process works in much the same way as any other process a professional would apply to a problem he or she encounters. There are three primary problems most readers face when confronting a difficult reading assignment.

1. Keeping their attention focused for the entire reading

2. Comprehending the details and intricacies of the material

3. Recalling the material for an assignment of exam

You cannot resolve these issues every time you sit down to read nor can you solve every math problem you come across. The better readers are not necessarily the ones who seem to have an easy time making it through their classes. Some students have an easier time making it though certain classes for any number of reasons. In some cases, the material is something they are already familiar with from previous classes or experiences, while in other cases they could just be gifted in that subject area. Finding certain classes easier than others does not make someone a good reader, however. The better readers are those who can apply themselves and do well when the readings are difficult and the material is unfamiliar.

First Stage: Previewing and Planning

Take some time before you being reading or studying to plan out your immediate goals for the time you are going to spend studying. This should not take more than a moment or two. Just think through what you are about to undertake and how it fits into the larger picture of what you are preparing to accomplish over the next few days or week. If you are about to begin a reading, consider the other demands on your study time right then. Are there other assignments you should be concerned about? Which assignments are most important? Which ones need immediate attention and which ones need the most work? You may have an essay due in a week and need to begin work on that right away, but you might also have a quiz tomorrow in another class.

Balancing the conflicting demands of college is a major part of getting through college. Doing this takes daily and weekly moments of consideration and reflection to ensure that you are using your time effectively and know how the work you are doing fits into the framework of a day, week, month or year.

When you begin a reading, take a moment to look over what you are about to read. Consider how long it is going to take to finish the chapter or assignment. Glance over the headings and the pictures and anything else that catches your eye.

This stage of the reading process should not take more than a few minutes, but it is very important to ensuring you remain focused and retain the material. The few minutes you spend going over a reading allows your mind to become familiar with the structure of the material. The preview establishes a set of expectations in your mind for what the reading is going to cover, and those expectations allow you to stay focused far better than if you had little foresight into where the reading is going. When you are half-way through a reading, your mind is better able to connect the material you have read with the expectations you have for the coming pages. The process of comparing where you have been to where you are going allows you to put the material together into a better format within your memory.

Reflection 2-6

1. Take a look at a chapter from one of the textbooks you are reading in another course. Is the topic of the course and the textbook one you are familiar with or is it new to you? How much do you know about it?

_____

_____

_____

_____

2. Glance over the headings, pictures and any questions they might have at the beginning or end of the reading. Without reading the chapter, write a summary of what you think the chapter will be about

_____

_____

_____

_____

_____

_____

_____

_____

_____

Second Stage: Reading Actively

Reading actively means reading thoughtfully and carefully. Treat any reading as a conversation with the author because that is really what it is. The author of any book you are reading sat down at some moment in time and considered what would be useful, informative, persuasive or entertaining to you. Reading the book the author wrote is part of your response to the conversation the author undertook with from a distant place and often a very distant time.

When you read, you need to have something to write with on the text itself. This could be a highlighter, a pen or a pencil. Anything you are comfortable with will do. The colors of highlighters allow you to recognize important sentences easily and to make distinctions on the text with the different colors. Their size, however, makes them a little more difficult to write comments in the margins. Other people prefer pens or pencils since they are easier to use when writing notes or making marginal comments and can be used for underlining. In the end, both approaches work quite well because both approaches keep your attention focused on the material and allow you to bring out the structure of the reading. What matters most is that you establish a systematic approach to your reading and learning.

Do not expect to figure out the best approach to reading right away. Your first semester in college is a good time to work out your methods for studying and to figure out which methods work best in which situations and for which courses. A system of color-coded highlighters and flash cards might work well in a biology class, but a black pen and marginal notes might be more effective in a history or literature course. As you learn, you will begin to figure out the best ways for you to learn and to teach yourself.

Looking Forward

When you are reading, you mind starts to predict where the reading is going next. The ability to anticipate is one of the distinct characteristics of the human brain and is what enables it to make rapid decisions, often much more rapidly than computers. As you follow the thinking process of the author, you mind automatically eliminates unreasonable possibilities from where the reading could go next in the coming paragraphs and pages. It simultaneously starts to predict where the reading actually will go.

This unconscious tendency to predict is not unique to reading, however. It is something the mind does when it is navigating any complicated situation and needs to anticipate what is coming up. When you are driving in heavy traffic, you are automatically making a number of predictions about how cars will behave. When playing checkers or chess, you cannot help but think through the next moves your opponent might make. When speaking with someone about an important topic, you start anticipating what the other person is about to say. (Hopefully you do not complete too many sentences for the other person.)

The ability to predict comes from the knowledge you have already assimilated and made a part of your consciousness. If you have a significant amount of knowledge about a certain topic or activity, your mind is better able to predict what is going to happen next. In situations where you have limited or no background knowledge, your ability to anticipate what will be said or happen next is greatly impaired. In these situations, it is common to feel nervous or uncertain and to want to avoid them in the future. Students often become anxious in situations where they do not know what is going to be on a test or when they are unsure of their writing skills.

When you are dealing with a reading that comes from a subject that you know very little about, you should focus on making sure you know how one piece of the reading fits with the next piece. Try not to be intimidated if some of the points and ideas simply do not make sense at first. Struggling with new ideas is part of learning.

Part of why previewing a reading is so important is that it activates the background knowledge you have about a topic. Your brain literally starts circulating blood more actively in the areas where any background knowledge about the topic is stored. The stage of previewing also allows you to get a good sense of where the reading is going. This stage is especially important when you are undertaking a reading from an unfamiliar area of study.

Looking Back

While you are reading, be sure to keep an eye on how well you are staying focused and how well you are comprehending the material. Even expert readers lose their focus while reading at times and struggle with difficult passages at other times. The best readers are not the students who read with ease. The best readers

94

know how to handle different and difficult materials and they do so in a systematic way.

Nearly everyone loses track of what they are reading at times. If the reading is more challenging, this is far more likely to happen since your short-term memory is being taxed to its limit and wants to rest.

When you discover that your mind has drifted, you must go back to the last sentence, paragraph or page that this began. Continuing to read without looking back is tempting, especially when time is short, but this creates even bigger problems. Skipping sections just makes the rest of the reading more difficult since you are lacking information the author assumes you already understand. You are also much more likely to forget the material of the chapter because it is going to be even more difficult to comprehend the structure of the reading when you did not understand whole sections if it. Taking the time to look back to those forgotten paragraphs makes reading the subsequent paragraphs far easier and that saves you time and frustration in the long run.

If you are taking notes or highlighting as you read, you can catch yourself drifting off very quickly. If a paragraph or two passes by without you marking your text, then you know your attention is drifting. But if you are commenting on the text as you read, it is far less likely that you are going to drift off in the first place.

Reflection 2-7

1.Write a quick outline of what you have read in this chapter so far.

_____

_____

_____

_____

_____

2. Write a quick outline of what you will be reading in this chapter.

_____

_____

_____

_____

_____

3. How do you think taking the time to review what you have read and preview what you are going to read is helping you recall the chapter?

_____

_____

_____

_____

_____

Stage Three: Reviewing What You Have Read

When the material has been covered and marked up systematically, taking a moment to review your notations and main ideas reinforces the important points and gives you a chance to take a broader look at the material. The review takes only a few minutes, but it makes an enormous difference in how well you are able to recall the material.

While you are reading, you mind focuses primarily on making sense of the details. It is difficult to step back when you are working through the smaller pieces of the reading and consider how the paragraphs fit within the larger framework of the reading. During the review, you can consider how all the paragraphs of the reading fit together and work with each other.

The review of the material should take place soon after you have completed the reading. Reviewing the material the next day is often a good idea since it is still relatively fresh in your memory, but distant enough to benefit from the rehearsal. The review allows you to renew the connections that the night's sleep has allowed to fade, and, once renewed, the connections are more likely to take root in your long term memory.

When you think back to how working memory and long term memory function, the reading process makes more sense. Your working memory can handle only so much material at once. Keeping the focus on the details rather than the bigger picture allows your working memory to apply itself more effectively to comprehending what you are reading at the time. Assembling the material into a unified and rational whole is quite challenging and cannot be done as well when you are focusing on the details of a difficult reading. Taking a few minutes after the reading is done allows your working memory to apply itself to figuring out the structure of the reading and to determine how it fits together and even how it can be applied to other areas of your life. Keeping these distinct tasks separate allows your working memory to function more effectively.

It is very important to keep the preview and review stages of the reading process simple. The easy habits are the ones you are more likely to retain. Making your study routines into complex undertakings might make your study time more effective at first, but it also makes them more time consuming and difficult to incorporate into your study routines. Simplicity is essential.

Reflection 2-8

Take a chapter from one of the textbook chapters you have read in another class and outline it from the headings and from your memory of the content of each section. The outline does not need to be too formal.

_____

_____

_____

_____

_____

_____

_____

_____

_____

_____

_____

_____

_____

_____

_____

100

Supporting and Using Your Reading

Much of the lecture and discussion that take place in class, prepare you for the reading. Instructors often use class time not for repeating a reading assignment but to either cover general points related to the reading or to go into more depth on certain selected points. The content of class lectures and discussions often acts as either a preview for a reading that develops your background knowledge or a review and reorganization of the materials it covers.

Using Class Notes

In many classes, professors use lectures to review and expand upon the textbook reading and to emphasize certain points. There are usually a few points the professors cover that are not covered in the textbook, but a good deal of the time is spent reviewing and giving examples of the topics covered in the textbook. In such classes, taking careful notes is important since the lecture reinforces the materials covered in the textbook chapter or reading assignment. But careful notes do not need to be highly detailed. In fact, taking too many notes can create confusion. Instead, try to pay attention to the structure of the lecture materials and note how points in the lecture are connected to each other.

In other classes, the professor assumes you can teach yourself from the textbook, and he or she spends class time introducing new material rather than reviewing what the readings or textbook cover. Such courses can be challenging. You must rely on your own abilities to make it through the reading materials, but if you apply your skills, these classes are not as difficult as they might appear.

Strategies for Testing

When you become aware of a test, set up a schedule to guide your preparations. Students who plan poorly for a test often delay and hope for a multiple choice test and a good deal of luck. Such hopes usually do not work out for the best. First of all, most instructors know how to write questions that distinguish students who know the material from students who do not. During multiple choice tests the student has no control over the material they have to cover. During essay exams, you have much more control over how the question is answered and how you can demonstrate what you understand.

In most multiple choice tests, the instructor wants you to know the material as it has been presented. There is usually no wiggle room for different interpretations. When preparing for a multiple choice text, your first priority needs to be comprehending and memorizing the material. Plan to finish the reading more than one day in advance of the test and take careful notes regarding any important points that come up. Take care to learn all specialized vocabulary terms since these words often end up on tests.

Spend the day before the test reviewing the materials once again. This rehearsal of the reading allows your memory to latch onto the structure more securely and also ensures that the details are easier to recall. The structure of the ideas is reinforced and you get a better perspective on how the elements of the reading fit together. Understanding the logical succession of ideas makes recalling the details much easier.

Reflection 2-9

1. What readings do you need to complete in this class and others for the next week or two?

_____

_____

_____

_____

_____

2. How much background knowledge do you have for each reading?

_____

_____

_____

_____

_____

3. What kinds of assignments are you going to be asked to complete in response to each of the readings? Tests, essays, etc.?

_____

_____

_____

_____

_____

104

Word Structure List 2

Exercise 1: Turn the following Greek and Latin word parts into flash cards. Put the word structure part on one side and the definition with an example on the back.

1. anti–against, opposite. Examples: antiestablishment, anticlimactic.

2. anthrop–human, mankind. Examples: anthropology, philanthropic.

3. arch/archi–chief, principal Examples: architect, archenemy, archetype.

4. bene/bon–good, well. Examples: beneficial, bonus.

5. cent–one-hundred. Examples: cent, century.

6. col, com, con, cor–together, with. Examples: collateral, communication, connect, correlation.

7. contra–against. Examples: contradict, contraction.

8. crat/cracy–to govern Examples: democracy, theocracy, autocracy.

9. de–away, off, down, reversal Examples: descend, detract, defile.

10. dec/deci–ten. Examples: decimal, December.

11. duc/duct–lead. Examples: induce, deduce, Ducate.

12. dys–faulty Examples: dysfunction, dystopia, dyslexia.

13. e, ex–out, former. Examples: emit, exterior.

14. equ–horse, equal. Examples: equestrian, equation.

15. fra/frac/frag–to break Examples: fraction, fragile, infringe.

16. gen–birth, kind, race. Examples: genesis, genealogy.

17. geo–earth. Examples: geothermal, geography.

18. log, loqu –reason, speech. Examples: logical, epilogue.

19. mille/milli–one-thousand. Examples: millimeter, million.

20. mis–bad, poor. Examples: mismanage, misappropriate.

21. port–carry. Examples: port, portable.

22. pos–place. Examples: post, position.

23. terra–land, ground. Examples: terrier, terra firma.

24. viv–live. Examples: vivisection, vivid.

25. voc–call, voice. Example: vocation, vocalist.

Word Parts Exercise 2

Directions: Underline the Greek or Latin word part and give a definition of the Greek or Latin word part. Do not define the word.

1. _____ misappropriate   _____ anticlimactic

2. _____ loquacious   _____ anthropomorphic

3. _____ geothermal   _____ emissary

4. _____ Genesis   _____ equestrian

5. _____ proportion   _____ fraction

6. _____ terrier   _____ million

7. _____ vivacious   _____ decode

8. _____ Ducate   _____ collaboration

9. _____ contravene   _____ beneficent

10. _____ centimeter   _____ decibel

108

Chapter 3

Developing a College Level Vocabulary

110

The Language of Educated People

When you come across a word you are not sure of, what do you do? Do you ever wonder where words come from and how they made it into the English language?

Most people skip the word with the hope that it really is not all that important. Doing so is always a mistake. Some take the time to loop up the word in a dictionary, but even that can be a mistake at times. Dictionaries can be quite useful in many cases, but there are other ways of figuring out the meanings of words that can be applied more rapidly and often more accurately.

Learning new vocabulary is not the primary purpose of reading college materials. The ideas and content of the essay or chapter should be your primary focus, but understanding the ideas and concepts without having a functional understanding of the vocabulary the author is using leaves you with gaps in your comprehension. The more difficult words usually play a key role in constructing the most important ideas. There is also a very good chance that the difficult vocabulary is part of the specialized vocabulary the professor intends to test you on in the coming weeks.

As a college student, you are in the process of joining an educated class of professionals. This class is not comprised of some elite group that controls the world from behind a curtain, but is instead made up of people just like you who have developed the ability to read and to use a more sophisticated vocabulary to communicate in a more precise and effective manner. They understand the more advanced ideas and concepts that influence our world and know how to use the language to explain and develop these ideas and concepts.

In colleges and universities, each field of study carries with it a specialized vocabulary that is used by the experts within the field. The obscurity of many of the words makes them difficult to understand for most students unfamiliar with the field. The authors are not inventing new words for the sake of frustrating you. Some professors might delight in creating problems for you, but the language you find perplexing at times is usually used in a precise manner by those who understand the complexities of the material. Learning to work out the more advanced vocabulary you come across in your college years is what this chapter is all about.

Four Ways to Learn New Words

Learning new words is not a simple matter of spending a lot of quality time with a dictionary. In fact, dictionaries should not always be the first choice when you come across a new word. Keep in mind that you are not reading to learn new words; you are reading to learn the content of the material. Taking time to look up a new word with each and every page makes it difficult to follow the material you are reading, especially if the content of the material is already difficult to follow.

There is no single method for learning new vocabulary. Instead, there are four methods, and you need to know how and when to use them:

1. Context clues
2. Word structure
3. Dictionaries
4. Flash cards

The better readers know how to use each of these, but they also know which method to use in which situation.

Context Clues

Many words can be figured out using the phrases and sentences surrounding the unfamiliar word along with your own good sense of what it could mean. Taking a moment to figure out what a word could reasonably mean is actually how you picked up most of the vocabulary you currently use each and every day. You did this automatically when you were a child and learning hundreds and sometimes thousands of words each year, and you did not do this by looking up words in the dictionary.

From the time you began listening to those around you, the context of words gave you clues to the meanings of those unfamiliar words you heard, but this was done with little conscious effort on your part. The ability to learn words from their context is the same skill you need now as a college student, but now the skill must be applied consciously and deliberately and to written words rather than spoken ones.

When you come across an unfamiliar word, try to act as if the word is not there, but is instead a blank needing to be filled in with another word or phrase. In some cases, figuring out the meaning of the word is easy. Writers are usually aware of which words are more difficult for their readers and often provide a phrase or synonym right next to the difficult word.

In other cases, you can rely on the sentences surrounding the word to give you a reasonable indication of what the word could mean. Do not worry too much about getting the exact definition of the word. Keep in mind that you are not reading for the sole purpose of learning new vocabulary. Instead, try to come up with a reasonable approximation of what the word means, write it in the margin of the paragraph and keep reading. In most cases, you are going to come up with a definition that is close enough to the word's actual meaning. Other times you might miss the definition, but a few misses should not cause too many problems with your comprehension of a reading. Frequently stopping to look up a word in the dictionary or skipping the words entirely does compromise your ability to understand a reading.

Exercise 3-1

Directions: Use the context of each <u>underlined word</u> to come up with a reasonable

definition. Write each definition in the margin of the article.

What Happened to Regulatory Reform

by Devin Leonard. January 30, 2010 in *The New York Times*.

1. Nearly two years ago, as a presidential candidate, Barack Obama gave a stirring speech at Cooper Union in New York about the need to reform the country's financial system. Joseph E. Stiglitz, the Nobel-winning economist, recalls it <u>fondly</u> in his powerful new book, "Freefall: America, Free Markets, and the Sinking of the World Economy.

2. But Mr. Stiglitz <u>laments</u> that the president failed to make good on such soaring rhetoric. He argues that Mr. Obama has continued for the most part to pursue the failed policies of George W. Bush. This, in the economist's view, has benefited Wall Street but has done little for ordinary citizens.

3. The results speak for themselves, Mr. Stiglitz says. He worries that "the best that can be said for the economy was that by the fall of 2009 it seems to be at the end of a freefall, a decline without an end in sight. But the end of freefall is not the same as a return to <u>normalcy</u>."

4. That raises a question: How is it that Mr. Obama the candidate understood the need for economic reform while Mr. Obama the president became a defender of the <u>status quo</u> in many unexpected ways?

5. Mr. Stiglitz, a former chief economist at the World Bank who spent time in the White House as an adviser to President Bill Clinton, thinks he knows the answer. He writes that Mr. Obama surrounded himself with an economic team whose members have been reluctant to <u>revamp</u> the financial system.

From   http://www.nytimes.com/2010/01/31/business/31shelf.html?ref=books

116

Word Structure

Most of the words that cause students trouble were created in during or in the centuries after the Renaissance when words were being constructed out of Greek and Latin prefixes and roots. There is a core set of prefixes and roots that come up again and again. This list might seem long, but the number of words the list opens up is many times longer. Once these prefixes and roots are committed to memory, they can be applied to new words rapidly.

Take a look at these words:

- Octogenarian

- Neonatal

- Precambrian

- Archbishop

You might be familiar with some or all of these words, but most college students would have some difficulty defining all of them accurately. You could look the words up in the dictionary, but this would take a good deal of time, and you really should stay focused on the reading itself as much as possible. The prefixes and roots of these words are actually quite common and show up in a great number of words. When you know the meanings of the prefixes and roots, you can make reasonable guesses at their meanings.

Take a look at these prefixes and roots and see if they help figure out the meanings of any of the words:

- oct—eight

- neo—new

- pre—before

- arch—first

If you were unfamiliar with the words, you could use the definitions of the prefixes and roots to form a reasonable guess about their meanings. If you were slightly familiar with the words, you might now be able to figure out more exacting definitions now.

Using the structure of the word to figure out its meaning works rapidly, more rapidly than context clues and far more rapidly than a dictionary. You do not need to take the time to look around a word and figure out its meaning, and you certainly do not need to spend any time flipping through a dictionary. You can see the prefix and the root and know its meaning immediately. The problem is that many words are not easy to figure out. Many words have one part that you know, but other parts are a mystery. In the word, "Precambrian," for example, it is easy to spot "pre" and know that it means "before," but what does "cambrian" mean? Then there are the cases where the parts of the word are clear, but the meaning simply does not follow what the parts of the word suggest. The month of October, for example, is not the eighth month of the year.

History has not been kind to many words in the English language. In many cases, words have undergone dramatic changes in their usage or have evolved spellings that obscure their origins. The month of October use to be the eighth month of the year until July and August were inserted in front of it and pushed it from the eighth to the tenth month of the year. The months of September, November, and December suffered from the same adjustment. The word "anticipate" was once spelled "antecipate" which showed that its prefix was once "ante," which means "before." It evolved into "anticipate" which changed its spelling but not its meaning. The prefix "ante" became "anti" which usually means "against" but, in this case, it retained the meaning "before."

The speed and ease of using word structure clues allows you to use them with little effort, but the confusion they can create means they should not be used carelessly. Instead, word structure should always be used in conjunction with context clues and your own good sense.

120

Exercise 3-2

Directions: Use the lists of Greek and Latin word parts at the end of this chapter and the previous two chapters. Underline the Greek or Latin prefix or root and then define the prefix or root next to the word. Do not try to define the word.

1. _____ anemia   _____ abhorrent
2. _____ antiestablishment   _____ missal
3. _____ beneficent   _____ micromanage
4. _____ biohazard   _____ pathetic
5. _____ centenary   _____ pedal
6. _____ immediate   _____ sextet
7. _____ dystopia   _____ valor
8. _____ decimate   _____ courtesan
9. _____ hypodermic   _____ vivacious
10. _____ polymorph   _____ sentence

1. _____ abnormal   _____ atheist
2. _____ archeology   _____ geothermal
3. _____ equestrian   _____ fidelity
4. _____ capricious   _____ confine
5. _____ corps   _____ portion
6. _____ theocrat   _____ audible
7. _____ extramarital   _____ dogmatic
8. _____ bellicose   _____ hyperbole
9. _____ dysentery   _____ hypoglycemic
10. _____ detract   _____ candor

122

Dictionaries

Dictionaries have long been touted as the source of word definitions, but the time it takes to find a dictionary and locate the word can make them something of a distraction from the reading rather than a resource. Many college dictionaries also provide several definitions for some words and choosing among them can create more confusion and waste time. The smaller dictionaries have precise definitions, but often do not have the more difficult words that you really need a dictionary for.

It is important to understand when to use dictionaries and which ones to use. If English is your second language, you probably find the smaller pocket dictionaries useful since they can be used rapidly and usually provide concise definitions. Most college students who can apply context closes and word structure reasonable well have little or no need for pocket dictionaries, but all college students should have a college dictionary available wherever they study frequently. You should use them primarily when you need a precise definition of a difficult word that cannot be reasonably determined from the context of through word structure clues.

Pocket dictionaries are used by second language students to check the meanings of common vocabulary terms they have not seen before and sometimes by English speaking students when they want to check the spellings of words they are not sure of. Their size makes them especially easy to use, but they also lack much of the specialized vocabulary most college students come across.

College dictionaries are about as thick as a brick and provide definitions of commonly used words and also the more difficult words that you really need them for. The sheer number of pages and the large number of definitions make using them time consuming, but they are the best source for the more difficult words you need to understand. Most college dictionary would, for example, have a definition of "Cambrian." College dictionaries are necessary for any college student, but they should be used primarily when exact definitions of difficult words are needed.

Historical dictionaries trace the changes a word has gone through over the decades and centuries of its existence. Few students need to have one readily available when they are reading, but many students find them useful when they are doing research and need to know how a word and its meanings have evolved over time. The most famous and extensive historical dictionary is the Oxford English Dictionary, which is several thousand pages in length and takes up more than twenty very large volumes in published form.

Reflection 3-3

1. Which dictionary or dictionaries do you have at home?

   _____

   _____

   _____

   _____

   _____

2. Do you have them near the area where you study? Why or why not?

   _____

   _____

   _____

   _____

   _____

3. Would you be more likely to use the internet or a dictionary to look up a word? Why? How long would each one take?

   _____

   _____

   _____

   _____

   _____

Exercise 3-4

Directions: Look up the following words in a dictionary that gives origins of words

1. Gelid.

Language of origin _____ Year of first use in English _____

Original definition _____

_____

Most recent definition _____

_____

2. Bellicose.

Language of origin _____ Year of first use in English _____

Original definition _____

_____

Most recent definition _____

_____

3. Wife.

Language of origin _____ Year of first use in English _____

Original definition _____

_____

Most recent definition _____

_____

Reflection 3-5

Directions: Suggest three words for the Dictionary. Spell the word, determine its part or parts of speech and define it. Then give its history as best you can and provide two examples of its use. One of the words can be a new usage of an old word.

1. _____

_____

_____

_____

_____

2. _____

_____

_____

_____

_____

3. _____

_____

_____

_____

_____

128

Flashcards

Textbooks often include a large number of specialized vocabulary words most students are not familiar with. Most textbooks use bold print to set the specialized vocabulary terms off from the rest of the text and provide a definition of the word nearby. These words make up the specialized vocabulary that experts use in the field covered by the textbook. Psychology, for example, has its own unique vocabulary that experts in the field use. Any psychology textbook includes these words in the text and provides exact definitions of how the words are used. There might be other possible definitions of the words available in a dictionary, but the textbook authors want you to know exactly how the word or phrase is used in a particular field of study.

The specialized vocabulary in a textbook is usually not too difficult to figure out but it is often quite difficult to memorize. Definitions of the words are usually provided right next to the word, and glossary in the back of the textbook usually covers all the new words covered in each chapter. Most instructors, however, require that you have not just a familiarity with the specialized vocabulary but a working knowledge of each word. This requires taking the time to memorize each specialized vocabulary word and its definition carefully.

After you finish a chapter in a textbook, go back over the chapter and compose flash cards for the words in bold. Knowing these words helps you understand the ideas of the chapter, and the accumulation of the specialized vocabulary develops your understanding of the field of study. Knowing the language of a field of study is essential to being knowledgeable about how people in that field construct their ideas and communicate with each other.

Exercise 3-6

Directions: Read the NY Times article carefully and complete the three following tasks:

1. Write a topic in the margin of each paragraph. The topic should be two to four words long and should give the basic point of the paragraph.

2. Define any words that are <u>underlined</u> according to their context and/or any word structure clues. (Some of the words that are underlined have word structure parts that have been covered in Word Structure List 1 or Word Structure List 2, so make sure you use these clues.)

3. Answer the questions at the end of the reading regarding the scientific nature of the study and the information.

October 9, 2009

Paper Challenges Ideas about 'Early Bird' Dinosaur

By John Noble Wilford

The "early bird" <u>archaeopteryx</u> may not be a bird, after all.

The first fossil of the raven-size species was an immediate sensation when it was <u>excavated</u> in 1860, in southern Germany. It had feathers and a wishbone, like birds, but teeth and a long, bony tail, like reptiles. Coming the year after publication of *The Origin of Species*, the discovery swayed many scientists into accepting Darwin's theory of evolution by natural selection.

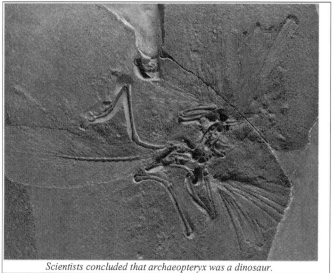

Scientists concluded that archaeopteryx was a dinosaur.

Thomas Henry Huxley, Darwin's staunch <u>ally</u>, recognized
the fossil in a limestone slab as a transitional species
between dinosaurs and birds. Over time, the 10 known
<u>specimens</u> of archaeopteryx became widely regarded as
examples of the earliest bird, which lived about 150 million
years ago.

Now scientists examining tiny pieces of a specimen's long
bone under powerful microscopes for the first time said they
found unexpected patterns <u>indicating</u> that the species grew
at a rate faster than living reptiles but only one-third as fast
as that of modern birds. The evidence, they reported
Thursday, challenges the <u>hypothesis</u> that archaeopteryx had
already developed characteristics of a physiologically
modern bird.

In a research paper being published in the online journal
PLoS One, the science team led by Gregory M. Erickson, a

paleontologist at Florida State University, concluded that archaeopteryx was simply a feathered dinosaur that might have been capable of some aerial behavior, though perhaps not powered flight. In short, despite feathers, it was not the archetypal bird.

Dr. Erickson said in an interview that studied under a polarizing microscope, the dense microstructure of the bone showed few traces of blood vessels. He said this was evidence of a slow metabolism by which the individual probably took more than two years to reach adult size. Birds have especially fast metabolisms, making them able to leave the nest in days or a few weeks.

Mark A. Norell, a co-author who specializes in dinosaur research at the American Museum of Natural History in New York, said the findings showed that "the transition to physiological and metabolic birds happened well after archaeopteryx." As a result, he added, the evolutionary emergence of birds "is still a huge mystery."

Both Dr. Norell and Dr. Erickson emphasized that their findings did not undermine the theory widely held among paleontologists that birds evolved from what are known as theropod dinosaurs. Birds, in that sense, are avian dinosaurs, although some ornithologists insist that is a stretch.

Paleontologists and ornithologists who had no part in the research said the findings were an important step in dinosaur-bird studies, but not surprising.

"Archaeopteryx has always been seen as a marvelous example of a transitional species," said Helen James, an ornithologist at the National Museum of Natural History in Washington. "You would expect to find its physiology to be transitional from what we see in modern birds and modern reptiles."

Lawrence M. Witmer, a paleontologist at Ohio University who conducts other archaeopteryx research, said that he was not surprised to learn that the species was "not fully avian," but that it had many features seen in later birds, indicating that it had not been displaced as "a very basal member" of the avian family tree.

In the new research, the scientists worked with Zhonghe Zhou of the Institute of Vertebrate Paleontology and Paleoanthropology in Beijing, conducting similar bone examinations on several specimens found recently in China of feathered dinosaur species. They concluded that confuciusornis was the first known species in which the transition to a bird's growth rate occurred.

Confuciusornis lived about 130 million years ago. Although its growth rate was somewhat slower than that of most same-size living birds, this species had no teeth, no long tail and seemed to grow more rapidly than archaeopteryx and other known specimens in between. More advanced bird fossils, with bones well supplied with blood vessels, appeared somewhat less than 100 million years ago.

In fact, it was the numerous discoveries in China that prompted the first close examination of archaeopteryx bones. Two years ago, Oliver W. M. Rauhut of the Bavarian State Collection for Paleontology and Geology in Munich gave the scientists permission to conduct the research on the museum's fossil, which like all the known specimens was of a juvenile.

Museum technicians extracted samples — hardly larger than specks of lint — from already damaged parts of a thighbone.

The bone growth rate, the scientists determined, was unbirdlike but reflected metabolic rates greater than those in non-dinosaurian reptiles; that is, they were more warm-blooded than coldblooded. In that respect, archaeopteryx appeared to be intermediate between reptiles and birds, growing at a probable rate close to that of marsupials, they said. Comparisons with other birdlike dinosaur specimens indicated that the bone structure of this archaeopteryx was not abnormal.

"Theories regarding the subsequent steps that lead to the modern avian condition need to be re-evaluated," the scientists concluded in the journal article, "to help understand what is turning out to be a complex evolutionary story."

136

Exercise 3-7

1. What did scientists find when they examined the bones of the bird fossil?

_____

_____

_____

_____

_____

2. Who conducted the research and where did they present their findings?

Why did they not present their research to the NY Times first?

_____

_____

_____

_____

_____

3. Why is the relationship between birds and dinosaurs considered a theory?

_____

_____

_____

_____

_____

Word Structure List 3

Exercise 1: Turn the following Greek and Latin word parts into flash cards. Put the word structure part on one side and the definition with an example on the back.

1. am–love Examples: amateur, amorous, amicable.
2. aud–hear. Examples: audition, audio.
3. auto–self. Examples: autonomous, automatic.
4. art–skill, craft Examples: art, artificial, artifact
5. corp–body. Examples: corporate, corpuscle.
6. cour, cur–run. Examples: course, current.
7. extra–outside of, beyond Examples: extraordinary, extrasensory.
8. fac/fic/fig–to do, to make Examples: factory, faction, fiction.
9. fore–before Examples: foresight, forgo, forebear.
10. fort–chance Examples: fortune, fortunate, fortuitous.
11. gram, graph–write. Examples: grammar, calligraphy.
12. hyper–above. Examples: hyperactive, hypersensitive.
13. hypo–below. Examples: hypothesis, hypoglycemia.
14. im, in, un–not. Examples: impossible, inability, unmanageable.
15. in, inte–in, within. Examples: inside, interior.
16. inter–between, among. Examples: internet, international.
17. micro–small. Example: micromanage, microscope.
18. mis, mit–send. Examples: missile, transmit.
19. mono–one. Examples: mononucleosis, monocle.
20. pent–five. Examples: pentagon, pentangle.
21. phon–sound. Examples: saxophone, phonograph.
22. poly–many. Examples: polynomial, polyglot.
23. semi–half. Examples: semiprecious, semi.
24. tetra–four. Examples: Tetris, tetracycline.
25. theo–god, religion. Examples: theology, theocracy.

140

Word Parts Exercise 3

Directions: Underline the Greek or Latin word part and give a definition of the Greek or Latin word part. Do not define the word.

1. _____ amiable   _____ artificer
2. _____ phonics   _____ monocle
3. _____ tetrarch   _____ audacious
4. _____ semitransparent   _____ courageous
5. _____ intermingle   _____ extraneous
6. _____ insensible   _____ telegram
7. _____ intense   _____ hypothesis
8. _____ micron   _____ impregnable
9. _____ forebear   _____ polymorphous
10. _____ corpulent   _____ theogony

142

Chapter 4

Topics and
Main Ideas

144

Topics and Main Ideas

The best readers are able to determine the topic and recognize the main idea of a paragraph readily. This might not seem to be that important of a skill at first, but the readers who struggle with college materials often find it difficult to discern what the author is writing about and how the ideas fit together. Understanding the topics and main ideas means understanding the ideas and their relationships to each other.

Getting to the main idea of a paragraph requires first being able to identify the topic of the paragraph and then being able to find which sentence makes the most important statement about that topic.

Developing a Notation System

A key to making your study time more effective is the development of your own notation system. Different people do like to study in different ways and in different environments, but there are elements that are common to all effective notation systems that students use.

Your notations should keep track of important points and should help you organize the new material in a way that is most useful for you and your goals.

- Specialized or important vocabulary.
- Main idea sentences
- Important details.
- Topics

- Interesting metaphors or images

- Reactions to controversial or unusual statements

Some people prefer o use a pencil or pen when notating in their readings since these are easy to write with and are easily found when needed, while other people prefer to use highlighters since they are brighter and easier to recognize on a page. Whether you use a pencil, pen, or colored highlighter is not important. That you develop a notation system that takes note of important elements of the reading and pulls out its structure is what matters. This can be done in many different ways, but it needs to be done if you are going to use your reading and study time effectively.

You may know of some successful students who never kept notes in their books. They might tell you that they never bothered with such silliness and you need not do so either. But there are also plenty of unsuccessful students who also never kept notations in their books. They might or might not tell you about their study habits, but it is quite likely that they did not have an effective approach to reading their textbooks. Keep in mind who is ultimately responsible for your success in college.

Developing a system of notations helps you study more effectively. It should not slow down your reading in any significant manner. A systematic approach to reading does not hurt your studying in any way. Developing your own method of reading is a far better approach than following the dubious approach of someone else.

Defining and Determining Topics

The topic of a paragraph is who or what the paragraph is about, and it acts as the paragraph's focal point. You can often find the topic stated in the opening sentence of a paragraph. In many paragraphs, it is repeated or referred to throughout the rest of the paragraph.

Being able to recognize the topic and taking note of it in each paragraph greatly increases you ability to focus your attention on the material. If you find that you have read a page or more without taking note of a topic in one of the paragraphs, you might be drifting off and losing your focus, and reading without focusing your attention on the material is a waste of time. Make a habit of writing a quick phrase in the margin of each paragraph you read, but be sure to do so quickly. It should not take more than a moment.

The topic should be stated in no more than a short phrase and sometimes as little as a word. The best topics are two to four words in length. One word topics seem to work well when paragraphs stand alone, but nearly all the readings you undertake as a college student are from essays and textbook chapters. A single word can rarely distinguish one paragraph from the next paragraph.

148

Take a look at the following paragraph:

> Isolated islands often support lone bird species. For example, the Galapagos hawk *Buteo galapagoensis* is the sole raptor on the semi-arid Galapagos Islands. In New Zealand, there are two diurnal raptors: the New Zealand falcon Falco novaeseelandiae in the forests and the swamp harrier *Circus approximans* in the open grasslands. The raptor with the most limited distribution is the endangered Hawaiian hawk *Buteo solitarius*, confined to one island.

Lone
bird
species

The topic of the paragraph could be "lone bird species." If "birds" alone were stated as the topic, it would be hard to distinguish this paragraph from the next paragraph, which would almost certainly address the topic of birds, and naming the individual species would take too long. In nearly all cases, two to four words is all it takes to list the topic, but notice that everything in the paragraph comes back to that simple phrase. The supporting sentences all go into greater detail, but they all describe certain species of birds that live alone on islands.

Exercise 4-1

Directions: Take a look at the following three paragraphs and see if you can determine the topics.

Raptors can be found in almost any habitat, from Arctic tundra to equatorial rainforest; arid desert to damp marshland; farmland to city. Because structural features of the habitat, rather than plant type, are most important to raptors, woodlands around the world tend to support a range of several different species. And raptors are not evenly distributed around the world: more than 100 species breed in the tropics, but only four in the high Arctic. Some habitats support raptors only at certain times of the year.

Some raptors can occupy a wide range of habitats, as long as there is suitable prey to catch. At the other extreme are the highly specialized species, dependent on a particular type of habitat. The snail kite Rhostrhamus sociabilis eats only snails, collecting them in the freshwater lowland marshes of Florida, Cuba, and Mexico, south to Argentina.

Each paragraph should have a different topic, which should allow you to take note of the progression of topics regarding raptors and their habitats. You were probably able to focus your attention on the material since you needed to extract that topic phrase. And if you needed to review this material for a test, you could easily glance over the topics and refresh your memory without having to reread each paragraph.

Identifying topics is the most important method for uncovering the structure of a more lengthy reading, but be careful not to work too hard on the topics. This might sound like odd advice, but the purpose of writing topics in the margins is to provide a check to make sure your attention is focused and to provide notes for later review. Longer topics of five to seven words are not more effective than shorter ones at accomplishing these goals. In fact, they soon begin to distract you from your primary purpose of comprehending the assigned reading.

Exercise 4-2

Directions: Write the topics for the following selection in the margins.

Male Chromosome May Evolve Fastest

By Nicolas Wade

Published: January 13, 2010 in *The New York Times*.

A new look at the human Y chromosome has overturned longstanding ideas about its evolutionary history. Far from being in a state of decay, the Y chromosome is the fastest-changing part of the human genome and is constantly renewing itself.

This is "a result as unexpected as it is stunning — truly amazing," said Scott Hawley, a chromosome expert at the Stowers Institute in Kansas City, Mo.

The Y chromosome makes its owner male because it carries the male-determining gene. Boys are born with one Y and one X chromosome in all their body's cells, while girls have two X's. The other 22 pairs of chromosomes in which the human genome is packaged are the same in both sexes.

The Y chromosome's rapid rate of evolutionary change does not mean that men are evolving faster than women. But its furious innovation is likely to be having reverberations elsewhere in the human genome.

152

The finding was reported online on Wednesday in the journal *Nature* by a team led by Jennifer Hughes and David Page of the Whitehead Institute in Cambridge, Mass. In 2003, Dr. Page, working with scientists at the Washington University School of Medicine, decoded the DNA sequence of the human Y chromosome. He and the same Washington University genome team have now decoded the chimpanzee Y chromosome, providing for the first time a reference against which to assess the evolutionary history of the human Y.

The chimpanzee and human lineages shared a common ancestor just six million years ago, a short slice of evolutionary time. Over all, the genomes of the two species are very similar and differ in less than 1 percent of their DNA. But the Y chromosomes differ in 30 percent of their DNA, meaning that these chromosomes are changing far faster in both species than the rest of the genome.

In the case of chimps, their mating habits are probably the source of the fierce evolutionary pressure on their Y chromosome. When a female comes into heat, she mates with all the males in the group, setting up competition within her reproductive tract between the sperm of different males.

Many genes that govern sperm production are situated on the Y chromosome, and any genetic variation that improves a chimp's chances of fatherhood will be favored and quickly spread through the population.

Sperm competition may have been important in the earliest humans, too, for some years after the chimp and human lineages split. Sperm competition could still play a role in human reproduction, some experts think, given the trickle of cases of heteropaternity, the birth of twins with different fathers.

Another reason for the intensity of selective pressures on the Y chromosome in both chimps and humans may be that natural selection sees it as a single unit, so a change in any one of its genes affects the survival of all the rest. On the other chromosomes, selection is more focused on individual genes because chunks of DNA are swapped between the members of each pair of chromosomes before the generation of eggs and sperm.

This DNA swapping process is forbidden between the X and the Y pair, keeping the male-determining gene from being transferred into the X chromosome, creating gender chaos. But this prohibition has caused most of the genes on the Y chromosome to decay for lack of fitness. In the rest of the genome, a gene damaged by a mutation can be swapped out for the good copy on the other chromosome.

154

In the Y, which originally had the same set of genes as the X, most of the X-related genes have disappeared over the last 200 million years. Until now, many biologists have assumed either that the Y chromosome was headed for eventual extinction, or that its evolutionary downslide was largely over and it has sunk into stagnation.

Dr. Page's new finding is surprising because it shows that the Y chromosome has achieved an unexpected salvation. The hallmark of the Y chromosome now turns out to be renewal and reinvigoration, once the unnecessary burden of X-related genes has been shed.

"Natural selection is shaping the Y and keeping it vital to a degree that is really at odds with the idea of the last 50 years of a rotting Y chromosome," Dr. Page said. "It is now clear that the Y chromosome is by far the most rapidly evolving part of the human and chimp genomes."

This does not mean that men are evolving faster than women, given that the two belong to the same species, but it could be that the Y's rate of change drives or influences the evolution of the rest of the human genome in ways that now need to be assessed. It would be "hard to imagine that these dramatic changes in the Y don't have broader consequences," Dr. Page said.

Andrew Clark, a geneticist who works on the Y

chromosome at Cornell University, said the Y's fast turnover of DNA could affect the activity of genes throughout the genome, because just such an effect has been detected in laboratory fruit flies.

The decoding of the Y chromosome's DNA was particularly difficult because the chromosome is full of palindromes — runs of DNA that read the same backward as forward — and repetitive sequences that confuse the decoding systems. Decoding the human Y took 13 years, and the chimp Y took eight years, Dr. Page said.

156

Distinguishing Specifics from Generalities

At times authors narrow their focus to make specific points while at others an author might move back and make more general statements about a topic. You might consider this to be similar to the different effects a film maker can bring about through close-ups and panning the horizon. One brings you in to examine a minute detail, while the other tries to give you the context for the situation.

Being able to recognize how details are collected under a single category is part of structuring readings in a way that can more easily be retained while and recalled later when you need to discuss or examine the material for a test or essay. Keep in mind how your memory holds onto material that is structured. If you are not able to distinguish between details and generalities, the materials will be more difficult to focus on while reading and impossible to recall later on.

Take a look at the following lists of words and phrases:

1. Ferrari	1. Books
2. Alfa Romeo	2. Pencils
3. Italian cars	3. Erasers
4. Maserati	4. School supplies

In both of these lists, one word or phrase is more general than the others, and the remaining three items are more specific. The relationship between the general terms and the specific terms is like a filing system where the file name is the more genera name or phrase, while the more specific items belong in the file.

158

Exercise 4-3

Directions: In the following lists, one word or phrase is more general than the other items in the list. Find that word or phrase and underline it:

1. Computer components	1. Time	1. Booties
2. Modem	2. Newsweek	2. Baby supplies
3. Keyboard	3. People	3. Diapers
4. Monitor	4. Magazines	4. Strollers

1. Chair	1. Mexican food	1. San Francisco
2. Desk	2. Burrito	2. Los Angeles
3. Office Furniture	3. Chorizo	3. Sacramento
4. Printer	4. Pan dulce	4. California Cities

Reflection 4-1

*Directions: If you had to remember all 24 items in the lists from **Exercise 3**, how would you go about doing so?*

_____

_____

_____

_____

_____

_____

_____

160

Main Idea Sentences

The same basic logic works of general and specific points works with sentences within paragraphs as well. Authors use more specific sentences at certain points to illustrate facts and ideas that require attention. At other times, they move back to provide general sentences to place those details within a context:

Take a look at the following groups of sentences:

1. Smaller mammals, such as meerkats, can easily be preyed upon when alone but can defend each other and their young when they are together and looking out for each other.

2. The confusion created by the scattering of a small group makes it more difficult for a predator to isolate one member of the group.

3. Most mammals are social and live in groups for the advantages the group provides.

4. For predatory animals, such as lions, working together in a group makes it possible for them to hunt more successfully and to keep what they have killed away from other predators.

Notice that the third sentence is more general than the other three sentences. It mentions that there are benefits of being a social mammal without describing any of the mammals or the benefits they gain from socializing. The other sentences go into detail and give examples of this main idea by describing various animals and the ways they are able to protect themselves or hunt more effectively in groups.

162

Exercise 4-4

Directions: Find the most general sentence of the four and answer the remaining questions.

Paragraph 1

1. The Mojave Desert lies just east of the San Bernardino and San Gabriel Mountain ranges and is home to several unusual species of plants and animals.

2. The kangaroo rat is a small rodent who survives in the dry heat of the desert by spending the days burrowed underground to avoid the heat and by expresses a powdery substance instead of urinating water to avoid losing any precious water from its body.

3. The Joshua tree is not a cactus but is part of the yucca family of plants and protects itself from the damaging effects of the sun by holding onto its dead fronds which add layers of protection.

4. The desert tortoise moves slowly which makes it easy for coyotes and other predators to catch it, but its ability to retreat into its shell makes it difficult, if not impossible, for those most predators to harm it.

1. Which sentence do you think is the main idea? _____

2. Why did you choose that sentence?

_____

_____

_____

Directions: Find the most general sentence of the four and answer the remaining questions.

Paragraph 2

1. Columbus believed that the islanders could be easily converted to Christianity because they did not have a well-developed religion of their own.

2. The islanders, he noted, had no advanced weaponry and knew nothing about modern warfare.

3. Columbus first arrived at the island of San Salvador on October 12, 1492 and began planning to take over the island and its people soon after.

4. He took a small number of them back to Spain by force.

1. Which sentence do you think is the main idea? _____

2. Why did you choose that sentence?

_____

_____

_____

Identifying Main Idea Sentences in Paragraphs

The main idea of the paragraph is the primary idea of the paragraph. The rest of the sentences in the paragraph support or describe the main idea by providing detailed explanations of the main idea. While supporting details tend to be specific or concrete, main ideas tend to be general and more abstract, which can make them more difficult to remember. The more specific and concrete details are usually more interesting and can be easier to recall by themselves, but the main ideas are what give the reading its structure, and understanding them together and how they relate to each other makes comprehending the entire chapter possible.

To see how a main idea functions differently from specific details, take a look at the following paragraph:

All frogs are carnivores, and many are generalized feeders that will take whatever small animals–vertebrates or invertebrates–their capacious mouths can accommodate. Relatively few frogs are large enough to eat other vertebrates, so most of them eat insects and other arthropods, and earthworms. But a large frog such as the North American bullfrog *Rana catesbeiana* can take birds and mice, small turtles and fish, and under crowded conditions is a fearsome predator on smaller frogs of its own and other species. Tadpoles for the most part are vegetarians–filtering organisms from the water, scraping algae from stones, consuming bottom debris. Some species have predaceous tadpoles, however, which capture invertebrates or other tadpoles. (*The Encyclopedia of Animals*. Fog City

Press, 2002)

Many would consider the sentence on the North American bullfrog and its ability to consume birds, mice, fish and turtles to be the most interesting sentence. But the paragraph is really not about the eating habits of just one frog. The paragraph is really about the carnivorous eating habits of most frogs and not just the abilities of one frog to consume larger animals. The first sentence describes all frogs as carnivorous and that sets up the sentences that follow. That makes the first sentence the main idea.

When you are trying to distinguish the main idea from the supporting details, try to determine which sentence presents the broadest point, the point that bring together the rest of the sentences in the paragraph. The topic of the paragraph is either the subject of the main idea sentence or else it is mentioned somewhere else in the sentence. In most textbooks, the authors place the main idea in either the first or second sentence. This format is preferred because it makes the structure of the paragraph more obvious to the reader. Do not, however, expect this to be the case in all paragraphs. The main idea can easily appear in the middle or at the very end of a paragraph.

Exercise 4-5

Directions: Find the most general sentence and underline or highlight it. Then explain how it organizes the each paragraph's supporting details.

Paragraph 1

Interesting names, many of which you are familiar with from other species, are applied to pinnipeds. A large group is a herd, but a breeding group is a rookery. Adult males are bulls, while females are cows but newborns are called pups in most species but calves in walruses. Between about 4 months and 1 year the young are described as yearlings and a group of pups is a pod. Immature males are bachelors. (The Encyclopedia of Animals. Fog City Press, 2002)

Why did you choose that sentence?

_____

_____

_____

Paragraph 2

The seven species of griffon vultures (genus *Gyps*) are usually numerous, and several hundred may gather at a food supply. The cinereous vulture *Aegypius monachus* is usually dominant over other vultures bickering at a carcass; its powerful bill enables it to eat coarse tissue, tendon and skin. The Egyptian vulture *Neophron percnopterus* cracks eggs and eats their contents; it picks up stones and hurls them at eggs too large to pick up and drop. Bones and tortoises are dropped from a height repeatedly by the bearded vulture *Gypaetus barbatus* which swoops down to eat the fragments; its habitat is open mountainous country from Spain to Central Asia. The unusual palmnut vulture *Gypoheirax angolensis* of Africa is dependent on the fruit of the oil palm. (The Encyclopedia of Animals. Fog City Press, 2002)

Why did you choose that sentence?

_____

_____

_____

Paragraph 3

For most amphibians and reptiles the abilities to see, hear and smell are essential for survival. The importance of each relates to the habits and habitats of each species. In frogs where the males attract the females by calling them, hearing needs to be acutely tuned to distinguish the calls of individual males from the noise of other males of the same or different species. Many male lizards use colors, sometimes subtle and sometimes brilliant, to attract females and warn other males to stay away from their territories. The sense of smell is often employed by collecting minute particles from the air with the tongue and passing them onto the olfactory senses in the roof of the mouth. (The Encyclopedia of Animals. Fog City Press, 2002)

Why did you choose that sentence?

_____

_____

_____

Paragraph 4

Rodent populations are subject to considerable fluctuations in numbers. Among the best-known examples are the cyclical peaks of north temperature voles and lemmings, which occur every three to four years. In the increase phase of the cycle, the breeding season is protracted and breeding activity at a maximum. At the peak, the breeding season is abbreviated and juvenile mortality high. Food becomes short, environmental stresses set in, and the population begins to decline. An eventual recovery of the population follows but with the genetic traits of those who were best able to survive the environmental stresses of the previous generation. (The Encyclopedia of Animals. Fog City Press, 2002)

Why did you choose that sentence?

_____

_____

_____

Paragraph 5

The mechanism of adhesion poses a special problem when the gecko is walking. In order to lift the foot a gecko must depressurize its blood sinus and the network of blood vessels and break the weak bonds that hold the setae to the surface. This is accomplished by rolling the toes up from tip towards the base, thus forcing blood back toward the foot and peeling the setae away from the surface. All of this happens with every single step the gecko takes. (The Encyclopedia of Animals. Fog City Press, 2002)

Why did you choose that sentence?

_____

_____

_____

172

Using Main Ideas

Main ideas can be more difficult to remember since they tend to be more abstract than the supporting details. But main ideas provide the structure of any lengthy reading, and learning how the main ideas work together is essential to understanding the more complicated and challenging materials you are coming across in college.

Underlining the main ideas as you read each paragraph allows you to emphasize the structure of the ideas as you come across them and this allows you to see and remember how the points are presented throughout the chapter or reading. Readers who do not or cannot identify main ideas most often come away from a reading with a vague notion of how the ideas are related to each other and are much more likely to forget the material soon after reading it.

Skimming the main ideas allows you to recall the material quickly and reinforces the structure of the ideas with relatively little effort. If you want to hold onto the details and supporting details of a reading, the structure of the ideas needs to be understood first. The time it takes to identify and underline the main ideas is minimal, but the benefits to your reading and study time are enormous.

Main ideas provide the structure of a longer reading. Being able to determine them quickly allows you to see how one paragraph relates to the next and how the reading itself is structured. When you lose sight of the structure of a reading, it becomes very difficult, if not impossible, to follow the reasoning behind the reading.

Think back to the first chapter and why structure is so important to developing memory. When you can remember the structure of a reading, you can remember the details within that reading far better. Pulling out the main ideas is the most effective way to expose the structure of a reading, especially within textbook chapters.

When you are finished reading a chapter, you do not need to read it a second time. Just review the notes and topics you have written in the margins and read over the main ideas you have underlined or highlighted. Re-reading a chapter can improve you comprehension of a difficult chapter, but it is usually at the expense of a great deal of time. When you read a chapter carefully the first time and take note of the topics and main ideas as you read, you only need to review the notes you have taken to ensure that you are able to recall the material from the reading. Taking just a bit of extra time during the reading to take note of topics and to underline main ideas can save you a great deal of time and can make your study time more effective.

Be careful not to confuse transitional sentences with main ideas. Transitional sentences are stated at the beginning of paragraphs, and they are often quite general. The whole purpose of a transitional sentence is to move you from the topic on one paragraph to the topic in the next paragraph. They can often be quite useful for establishing the relationship between the two paragraphs, but, unlike main ideas, transitional sentences to do not set up the supporting details in the paragraph.

Incomplete or Unstated Main Ideas

All paragraphs have a point, but many of them do not have a main idea setting it out nice and clearly. In many types of writing, the details the writer provides imply an idea even when it is either only partially stated or not stated at all.

The main idea is still there and organizing the supporting details of the paragraph, but it exists between the lines and needs to be uncovered by you. Different readers are able to recognize the same essential main ideas, but they might use slightly different sentences when writing it out.

The two instances where you need to come up with a main idea come when the main idea is either incomplete or not stated at all.

Weak Main Ideas

Some paragraph have main ideas that come up short and simply do not hold the supporting details together effectively. These weak main ideas need to be completed after you go through the paragraph and determine how the supporting details related to each other.

The following paragraph demonstrates some of these issues:

Vultures are scavengers that rarely kill prey. They are incapable of sustained flapping flight and depend on rising air currents to keep them soaring aloft. Because of the vast distances they can travel in search of carcasses, they are exceptionally efficien and important scavengers. Most species have bare areas of skin on their head and neck, thought to reduce fouling of their feathers when feeding and perhaps to help with heat regulation. The seven species of griffin vultures (genus *Gyps*) are usually numerous, and several hundred may gather at a food supply.

Notice that the paragraph the first sentence does not act as a strong coordinating main idea. It makes a statement about vultures being scavengers that rarely kill prey, but the rest of the paragraph does not discuss scavenging in much detail or the rare instances of vultures killing prey. The paragraph, instead, goes on to focus on the distances the birds can travel and their lack of feathers on their head and neck. It also mentions how numerous griffin vultures can be.

A complete main idea for this paragraph should say something about the physical characteristics and social behaviors of these vultures. Something like this might do:

Vultures are scavenger with certain physical characteristics and social habits that distinguish them from birds who kill their prey.

The expanded main idea does not impose the reader's opinions on the material, but instead develops the main idea using the supporting details that are already in the paragraph.

Implied Main Ideas

In many paragraphs, the main idea is not stated in one sentence. Many paragraphs instead have what are called implied main ideas, which must be inferred from the sentence or sentences that are provided. Implied main ideas are most often used in non-textbook writing and especially in narratives, such as historical accounts, literary stories and even news reports, where the lessons of the paragraph is not stated directly but can be inferred from the details that are provided. The main idea instead could be made up of two sentences or it might be stated in an incomplete manner or it might not be stated at all and would be inferred from the details provided. This kind of writing requires that the reader be more involved in the organization of the main points since the reader must infer why the details matter.

Keep in mind that implied main ideas are still main ideas. They are a little tougher to identify, but there is a process for going about digging implied main ideas out of paragraphs.

1. Read the paragraph carefully,

2. Determine the topic of the paragraph and write it in the margin,

3. Ask yourself what you have learned about the topic.

Your answer should bring the details of the paragraph together in one sentence and should provide you with the main idea of the paragraph.

There are always going to be differences in how readers identify implied main ideas, but in most cases the basic points are going to be quite similar. The reader should, however, be quite careful with distinguishing between what the author's implied main idea is and what he or she as reader might personally think of certain facts. In other words, it is important to distinguish between your own opinions and what the author might be trying to demonstrate. It is not a matter of putting your own opinions aside to focus on the author's. Nor is it a matter of placing your own evaluation above that of the author's but of knowing the difference between what the author is trying to demonstrate and what your reaction to what is being demonstrated.

Here is a paragraph from Howard Zinn's *A People's History of the United States* where he provides a list of details about Spain's political situation as the time Columbus first encountered the Native American tribes:

> Spain was recently unified, one of the new modern nation-states, like France, England, and Portugal. Its population, mostly poor peasants, worked for the nobility, who were 2 percent of the population and owned 95 percent of the land. Spain had tied itself to the Catholic Church, expelled all the Jews, driven out the Moors. Like other states of the modern world, Spain sought gold, which was becoming the new mark of wealth, more useful than land because it could buy anything.

Notice that Zinn does not provide a main idea that holds the paragraph together. The first sentence mentions that Spain was unified and compares it to other

European countries, but it does not stick with that topic. Instead it goes on to add points about the land and wealth distribution and the expelling of Jews and Moors from the country. It also mentions the new focus on gold.

Though there is no clearly stated main idea, Zinn is trying to demonstrate a point about Spain at the time of Columbus' expedition. If we follow the three stages of determining the implied main idea, we should first identify the topic of the paragraph. Different readers might form slightly different topics, but most topics will be fairly similar. In this case, we could say the topic any one of these:

1. Spain unified but poor, or

2. Spanish political difficulties, or

3. Rich and poor in Spain.

Then we need to ask "What Zinn is trying to tell us about the topic?" We could come up with any of these answers:

1. Spain was unified by a wealthy and ruthless nobility who controlled the what was an otherwise poor country; or,

2. The nobility dealt with the Spanish political difficulties by expelling many ethnic groups and by exploiting the peasants; or,

3. The Spanish nobility were incredibly rich and sought gold while ignoring the poverty of the peasantry.

These main ideas might all be somewhat different, but they all bring the details together is fairly similar ways and catch the basic point Zinn seems to be making.

180

Identifying main ideas is not an exact science but is instead a necessary process of organizing the many details in a way that organizes the detail in a way that makes sense to you but also takes the author's intent into account.

Exercise 4-6

Directions: Read the following paragraph from Howard Zinn's People's History of the United States. *Follow the three steps of the process to determine implied main ideas and answer the questions that follow.*

Paragraph 1

So, approaching land, they were met by the Arawak Indians, who swam out to greet them. The Arawaks lived in village communes, had a developed agriculture of corn, yams, cassava. They could spin and weave, but they had no horses or work animals. They had no iron, but they wore tiny gold ornaments in their ears.

1.Topic _____

2.What is Zinn trying to show about this topic?

3. Implied main idea

_____

_____

Paragraph 2

On Hispaniola, out of the timbers from the Santa Maria, which had run aground, Columbus built a fort, the first European military base in the Western Hemisphere. He called it Navidad (Christmas) and left thirty nine crew members there, with instructions to find and store the gold. He took more Indian prisoners and put them aboard his tow remaining ships. At one part of the island he got into a fight with the Indians who refused to trade as many bows and arrows as he and his men wanted. Two were run through with

swords and bled to death. Then the Nina and the Pinta set sail for

the Azores and Spain. When the weather turned cold, the Indian

prisoners began to die.

1. Topic _____

2. What is Zinn trying to show about this topic?

3. Implied main idea

_____

_____

Paragraph 3

Trying to put together an army of resistance, the Arawaks faced

Spaniards who had armor, muskets, swords, horses. When the

Spaniards took prisoners they hanged them or burned them to

death. Among the Arawaks, mass suicides began, with cassava

poison. Infants were killed to save them from the Spaniards. In two

years, through murder, mutilation, or suicide, half of the 250,000

Indians on Haiti were dead.

1. Topic _____

2. What is Zinn trying to show about this topic?

3. Implied main idea

_____

_____

Strategies for Using Topics and Main Ideas

Certain types of readings or reading situations might require that you adjust or shift your reading strategy when it comes to identifying topics and main ideas. Some readings might be composed with short paragraphs of one to three sentences where there really is no stated main idea and trying to come up with implied main ideas would not be useful. This is common in journalistic writing, such as newspaper, magazine or blog writing. The articles are usually not more than one or two pages and do not have a complicated structure. They are still organized in a way the author wants you to recognize, but the article probably does not require the kind of attention to main ideas a textbook chapter would. In these situations, it would probably be better to focus on the topics of each paragraph rather than trying to deduce an implied main idea from a limited number of sentences.

In longer and more challenging readings, such as textbook chapters from either a sociology or chemistry class where you must understand how several different concepts are working together, identifying the topics would be useful for keeping your attention focused while you are reading, but you will also need to identify the stated main ideas for review after you have completed the reading. In these situations the structure of the ideas is essential to understanding the material. Keeping notes in the topics while identifying the main ideas would be useful for ensuring that you understand the material and can recall it well after reading it.

For extended narratives, such as novels or historical writings, the main ideas are often not supplied but the length of the reading necessitates that you understand its structure. In these situations, noting the topics would be necessary to keep your attention focused, but deriving implied main ideas and noting them in the margins would also ensure that you ware able to recall the structure of the narrative and the succession of the events in the material.

In each situation, you need to evaluate the reading before you begin to determine which approach is to work best while you are reading. Keep in mind that the goal is make sure that the time you spend on the reading is not wasted. Doing excessive work, such as composing implied main ideas for a one page news article, or doing sloppy work, such as reading a complicated textbook chapter on psychology while listening to your iPod and without taking note of the important vocabulary or main ideas. You will learn little from the textbook and almost certainly not be able to recall the important concepts you were supposed to learn. In both cases, you would be wasting your time by either doing unnecessary work or by doing things that make your work worthless.

The most effective approach is to decide on your strategy before beginning the reading. You will be able to determine if you need to keep your approach simple, such as just taking note of the topics, or if it needs to be more involved, such as keeping track of topics, main ideas and difficult vocabulary, by examining the type of reading you need to complete and what you need to get from it. This means using the preview stage of the reading process to determine how you are going to use topics, main ideas and implied main ideas during the second stage of the reading process.

Writing in Your Books

Most students have been taught never to write in their books. Librarians and teachers have driven this lesson into students' heads for the first 12 years of their education, and for good reason since the books are expensive to replace once their damaged. But in college the books you use for the classes are usually your books since you bought them. There is no need to replace them and you are probably not going to use them again after the semester is finished. It is best to use them well while you need them.

You might be able to sell them back to the bookstore at the end of the semester, but keeping them in pristine condition usually has little effect on their value.

Books should not be treated as if they were antiques. They are meant to be used and to use them well means writing on them. Some people think this is being disrespectful to the book, but the author's information and ideas are more important than the pages of the book and getting to a better understanding of what the author has written.

186

Reflection 4-7

1. Take a quick look over the article and decide which strategies you need to use while reading it. What type of approach is going to work best for this reading? Would a combination of strategies work?

_____

_____

_____

_____

_____

_____

_____

2. How familiar are you with the topic? Is there any difficult vocabulary? If so, what will you do with it?

_____

_____

_____

_____

_____

_____

_____

188

Exercise 4-8

Directions: Write the topics in the margin of each.

Three Desert Lizards Evolve White Skins

Through Different Mutations to the Same Gene

By Ed Yong

Posted at http://scienceblogs.com/notrocketscience on: December 28, 2009

In the White Sands National Park of New Mexico, there are three species of small lizard that all share white complexions. In the dark soil of the surrounding landscapes, all three lizards wear coloured coats with an array of hues, stripes and spots. Colours would make them stand out like a beacon among the white sands so natural selection has bleached their skins. Within the last few thousand years, the lesser earless lizard, the eastern fence lizard and the little striped whiptail have all evolved white forms that camouflage beautifully among the white dunes.

Erica Bree Rosenblum from the University of Idaho has found that their white coats are the result of changes to the same gene, Mc1r. All of these adaptations arose independently of one another and all of them reduce the amount of the dark pigment, melanin, in the lizards' skin. It's a wonderful example of convergent evolution, where

190

the same environmental demands push different species along the same evolutionary paths. But Rosenblum has also found that there are many ways to break a gene.

Each of the three lizards has a different mutation in their Mc1r gene, that has crippled it in diverse ways. These differences may seem slight, but they affect how dominant and widespread the white varieties are, and how likely they are to branch off into new species of their own. Even when different species converge on the same results - in this case, whitened skin - and even when the same gene is responsible, their evolutionary paths can still be very different.

The Mc1r gene encodes a protein called the melanocortin 1 receptor (MC1R). It's a messenger that sits astride the cell's membrane and transmits messages across it. It triggers a sequence of events that stimulates the production of the dark pigment melanin. In this way, it affects the skin colour of many animals and faulty copies of the gene tend to result in lighter colours. In humans, for example, around 80% of redheads owe their hair colour to common faulty variant of Mc1r.

In each of the White Sands lizards, just one of the MC1R protein's many amino acids has been swapped (red circles above), and it's a different one in each species. All three amino acids lie within the part of the protein that straddles the cell membrane. These regions are important for keeping the protein together, and for channelling signals from one side of the membrane to another.

Rosenblum found that white fence lizards and whiptails have MC1R proteins that are severely disabled by their single mutations. Their ability to channel signals across the membrane has been slashed by around two-thirds. In the fence lizard, the protein can't fit properly into the cell's membrane. In the whiptail, the altered protein doesn't interact well with partners that carry on the signals it transmits. Either way, there's a breakdown in communication.

The earless lizard is slightly different. Its MC1R protein worked in the normal way so the link between its replaced amino acid and the white colour isn't straightforward. It could be that a gene sitting very close to Mc1r is actually responsible for the colour change. Alternatively, it's possible that the protein works normally, but is much less stable, or produced at much lower levels. Either way, it's clear that all three lizards have achieved their adaptive camouflage through different means.

192

These adaptations must have been independent. The fence lizard and the whiptail are the most closely related of the pair, but even their last common ancestor still lived at least 175 million years ago. The White Sands dunes, on the other hand, have only been around for 6,000 years.

You might think that the means are unimportant if the ends are the same. As long as the lizards are white, does it really matter why they are white? Rosenblum certainly thinks so.

For a start, the whitening variants of Mc1r are inherited differently. The fence lizard's one is dominant, so even individuals with one copy have blanched skin. The whiptail's version, on the other hand, is recessive so it takes two to whiten. These different inheritance patterns also affect how widespread the whitening mutations are among the lizard populations. And they could affect the odds that the white versions will eventually branch off into isolated species. After all, these lizards use their colour patches to signal to one another, so whitening up for the sake of camouflage could affect their ability to recognise peers or attract mates.

Reference: Rosenblum et al. 2009. Molecular and functional basis of phenotypic convergence in white lizards at White Sands. PNAS doi:10.1073/pnas.0911042107

Exercise 4-9

Directions: Look over your topics and/or main ideas and any notes you took during the reading. Write a summary of the main points of the article using only your notations.

_____

_____

_____

_____

_____

_____

_____

_____

_____

_____

_____

_____

_____

_____

_____

_____

_____

194

Reflection 4-10

1. How well did your approach work at getting the main points of the article?

---

2. Was the article difficult or easy or somewhere in between?

---

3. Did you have trouble with the vocabulary? How did you deal with words such as "adaptations," "membrane," and "blanched"

Word Structure List 4

Exercise 1: Turn all of the following Greek and Latin word parts into flash cards. Put the word structure part on one side and the definition with the example on the back.

1. amb–to go, to walk   Examples: ambitious, ambulance.

2. ambi, amphi–both.   Examples: ambidextrous, amphibian.

3. anim–life, mind, soul, spirit   Examples: unanimous, equanimity, animosity.

4. card/cord/cour–heart   Examples: cardiac, courage, cordial.

5. carn–flesh   Examples: carnivorous, carnival, incarnation.

6. di, dis–away, not.   Examples: divorce, disapproval.

7. di/dia–apart, through   Examples: dialogue, diagnose, dialectic.

8. equi–even, equal.   Examples: equation, equitable.

9. eu–good, well.   Examples: eulogy, eugenics.

10. fab/fam–speak   Examples: fabulous, fame, infamous.

11. fer–to bring, to carry, to bear   Examples: offer, transfer, infer.

12. -logy–study.   Examples: sociology, geology.

13. mal–bad.   Examples: malicious, malaise.

14. meter, metr–measure.   Examples: speedometer, metric.

15. phil–love.   Examples: philanthropy, Anglophile.

16. phob–fear.   Examples: phobia, arachnophobia.

17. pro–before, in favor of, forward.   Examples: promote, professional.

18. pseudo–false.   Example: pseudo-intellectual, pseudo-science.

19. quad–four.   Examples: quadruped, quadrilateral.

20. quint–five.   Examples: quintuplets, quint.

21. re, retro–again, back.   Examples: rewind, retroactive.

22. scrib, script–write.   Examples: scribble, transcript.

23. sed, sess, sid–sit.   Examples: sedate, session, president.

24. super–above.   Examples: superior, super.

25. tri–three.   Examples: tricycle, trifecta.

198

Word Parts Exercise 4

Directions: Underline the Greek or Latin word part and give a definition of the Greek or Latin word part. Do not define the word.

1.	_____ malcontent	_____ transfer
2.	_____ proviso	_____ immunology
3.	_____ pseudonym	_____ philanthropy
4.	_____ quintuplets	_____ dialectic
5.	_____ transcribe	_____ euphemism
6.	_____ sedative	_____ equilateral
7.	_____ triumvirate	_____ fable
8.	_____ superlative	_____ division
9.	_____ revision	_____ anime
10.	_____ metronome	_____ carnal

Made in the USA
Las Vegas, NV
17 January 2021